PLANNING THE NEW OFFICE

Michael Saphier

PLANNING THE
NEW OFFICE

McGraw-Hill Book Company

New York   St. Louis   San Francisco   Auckland   Bogotá   Düsseldorf
Johannesburg   London   Madrid   Mexico   Montreal   New Delhi   Panama
Paris   São Paulo   Singapore   Sydney   Tokyo   Toronto

Library of Congress Cataloging in Publication Data

Saphier, Michael.
Planning the new office.

Includes index.
1. Office layout.   2. Business relocation.
I. Title.
HF5547.S28   658'.2   77-24367
ISBN 0-07-054721-1

234567890   VHVH   76543210

The editors for this book were Jeremy Robinson and Lester
Strong, the designer was Elliot Epstein, and the production
supervisor was Teresa F. Leaden. It was set in Optima by
University Graphics, Inc.

Printed and bound by Von Hoffman Press, Inc.

To RUTH who, having suffered
through one book, invited all
of the problems of a second
by not hiding my pad and pencil.

Contents

II PLANNING FOR THAT NEED

III APPLYING THE PLAN

IV DEVELOPING THE PLAN

Illustrations

Forms and Charts

Preface

Once upon a time there was a company president who sat in his office, answered his morning mail, made a few phone calls and a date for lunch, and then had nothing to do. He looked around his office and noticed that the walls needed painting, the carpet was worn, the furniture was shabby, and the windows were dirty. He buzzed for his secretary and dictated a memo to his vice president, saying, "Let's move!"

Actually I know of no company whose move was motivated in quite that way. But however it does come to pass, the simple phrase "Let's move," or "Let's redo our space," sets in motion a chain of events that can become one of the most rewarding activities a company can undertake or the most irritatingly unproductive one in which it has ever gotten involved. To make sure that it is rewarding and as problem-free as possible is the major purpose of this book.

Whatever it is that does set the chain of events in motion, relocation or renovation is peculiarly a prime function of management, and the end result is solely management's responsibility. Despite that fact, and despite the fact that the total project can be so costly, all but a handful of companies are equipped with in-house personnel capable of dealing with the innumerable day-to-day decisions that are part of each space-planning and design task.

Over the years tremendous changes have taken place in the kind of office buildings being developed, the systems and procedures under which businesses operate, and the kind and number of talents that have become part of the planning process. All these have added to management's problems in trying to cope with the questions about real estate, organization, operation, economics, construction, and aesthetics that must be answered in the normal course of any project.

Books on office planning have been written for the students and practitioners of space planning, architecture, real estate, and interior design. But even though the whole process of change is management's responsibility, there is no comprehensive manual that can help a company about to embark on an office-planning program. This book was written to fill that void. It could provide help before the need for a move becomes apparent. It should be able to help management pinpoint the need far enough in advance to allow for intelligent planning, and continue to be of help until the move is over, the space occupied, the last machine installed, and the last ashtray delivered.

I remember talking with an executive who admitted an inability to decide which space-planning company to hire because each seemed to offer the same talents and the same assurances of responsible performance, all for basically the same fee. He was jesting—but not entirely. This was one of the first in a long series of decisions that he would be called upon to make. He was as ill-prepared and ill-equipped to make that one as he would be to make most of the others that he would face throughout the project. Make them he would, however, and with luck, most of them would turn out well.

But over the years I have watched this decision-making process, have contributed my own input to it, and have seen how frequently it can go wrong. I saw how costly the errors could be and how unnecessary most of them were. There was, for example, the client who brought his financial advisor to the project much after the planning and designing had been completed and, on the cost-cutting suggestion of the advisor, eliminated a major visual aspect of the job. Approached earlier in project chronology, cost cutting could have been accomplished without any loss of essential design elements.

Another example was the client who made his decision on the advice of a realtor and so rented the wrong kind and amount of space for his needs. He made this basic, costly error because his rental commitment was made before his space needs had been properly analyzed.

Then there was the client who became the owner of a huge number of desks, none of which provided the proper work station for the tasks to be accomplished, because his decision to buy the desks was based on advice from a well-meaning manufacturer of office furniture, totally unfamiliar with the company's true operational requirements.

This book should go far to eliminate such "judgmental" errors. It should help the decision-making process by educating management as to the kind of information it will have to pass judgment upon and by exposing management to the variety of talents and professional specialties available to help it pass judgment. These specialties will vary with the size and scope of the project. The planner, architect, or interior designer (and sometimes all three talents) may be involved in the average project. In addition, help toward problem solving can come from specialists in material handling and paper handling, forms, filing, duplication and reproduction, word processing, communications, and data processing. The experience and particular knowledge of a furniture manufacturer or supplier, an equipment manufacturer, a sociologist, and a task analyst may be needed sometime during the development of the project. With the planning problem so very complex, the client's need for help is obvious. It becomes almost overwhelming when you look at a full list of the talents that may be called upon to complete a project. That list could include not only the specialists already named but also specialists in audio-visual systems, in-house feeding, medical advisors, building and equipment maintenance people, waste-handling and security specialists, plus, of course, both structural and mechanical engineers. In addition, no project really gets off the ground without real estate help, legal talent, financial input, construction management and control, repair and refurbishing service, insurance experts, moving aid, and, if everything goes well and everybody involved is proud of the end product, public relations help!

The best results will come from the interaction of these specialists—sharing their knowledge, their abilities, and their concern—in common effort, coordinated by management. A competent architect or designer or general contractor can usually solve his or her particular problem without help from any of the others. The difficulty comes in merging these efforts, while the penalties for not doing so grow constantly greater and greater.

The book was prepared to make management aware of its needs and familiar with the talents required to help meet those needs and, also, to show management how to organize that help and coordinate the knowledge it can supply. This is not a book on design or on real estate or on word processing. It is a book intended to tell management what the designer, the realtor, and the word-processing expert are supposed to do, and most important, how management must communicate with each of them to make what each does more meaningful in the total project.

Although no project ever really follows a clear-cut chronological pattern, this book is organized as closely as possible according to the way projects should be run. Each of the five sections is a major division, or phase, of a project, and each deals in depth with both the effort and knowledge required for the successful completion of that phase.

A word of warning: Section and chapter headings tend to give an illusion of the separation of talent responsibilities. No such separation actually exists. Over the years, as more and more specialties began to appear, filling valid needs in the ever-changing fields of office management, office organization, and office planning, each began to lose the sharpness of definition that separated one from the other. Where each had functioned independently, it became obvious that their interdependence, the pooling of their findings under intelligent guidance, had to work toward the benefit of the total project.

Section I evaluates the need for change and outlines the methods for arriving, as rapidly as possible, at conclusions sufficient for the preparation of a feasibility study. From this preliminary study the decision can then be made as to whether or not the project can and should be completed. This preliminary probe into the feasibility of the project is basic to the structure and the aim of this book: to avoid too great an expenditure of time and money before the validity of the project has been proved, but once proved to make sure that the best project results are attained. Despite the fact that the work, done to arrive at the tabulation of requirements and the financial analysis that make up the feasibility study, will be done rapidly, it will provide a thorough base for the effort to be followed in the next sections.

It would be wise for the user of this book to read the entire text before actually beginning the preparation of the feasibility study. Any subject covered in the preparation of that study will have its in-depth counterpart elsewhere in the book. Familiarity with all the aspects of a planning project—and with the structure of the book—will make the book simpler to use as a checklist to ensure as complete a feasibility study as possible.

The special talent and knowledge that can be helpful in each step along the way to project completion, the availability of that help from outside if it does not exist on client staff, and how to put it to best use is dealt with at the end of each section in an addendum entitled "Project Staffing." In it will be listed the kind of help, knowledge, talent, and/or professionals required for the performance of effort to be accomplished in that section. The described capabilities may be in-house help or outside consultants, and the mix will vary from company to company. The important part of these addenda is that they fully describe the effort needed, why each is needed, what can (or cannot) be expected from each kind of consultant, how someone practicing a particular specialty can be located, and generally what the costs or fee arrangements are. This knowledge is necessary for proper project planning and task assignment.

Sections II and III and the first chapter of Section IV cover some of the areas touched upon in Section I, but they deal in far greater detail with all of the study, analysis, exploration, evaluation, and decision making necessary for project success. The second chapter of Section IV and all of Section V deal with the implementation of the decisions made and their translation into the reality of a completed project.

Starting with an evaluation of the need for change and ending with a description of how to implement the plan developed to meet that need, this book attempts to give company management, and company consultants, complete information concerning all the aspects of office planning and moving. Some of the subjects talked about concern things that will not go through very radical changes from year to year. They include such documents as leases for space or contracts for consultants, space standards covering allotments of square footage to personnel for specific tasks, the worksheet forms, etc. The information about these is as all-inclusive as possible. Where the book deals with such things as rent schedules in various sections of the country, furniture costs, equipment performance, etc., all of which do go through frequent changes over the years, the sources for the rapid acquisition of up-to-date information on each of these subjects are listed for the reader's use.

For the reader interested in further details on any of the subjects touched upon in this book, there is a "For Your Information" list at the end of the text which catalogs books and magazines that may be worth reading and associations and societies that may be worth contacting for additional material and information. Also, after the main text, there is a comprehensive list of the things to be done during relocation. This can be an invaluable aid in the preparation of a step-by-step checklist for any specific project.

Most of the forms shown and suggested for use in conjunction with the work outlined in Section I have been created to fill an obvious need. The vast majority of companies contemplating a change have no such documents to help them find their way toward the decisions that must be made. The suggested forms, with whatever applicable modifications the user feels should be made, will do much to pinpoint the problems if they exist or prove that there are no problems. Once a move has been made, the final forms and worksheets should become a permanent inventory. Kept up-to-date always, they will be available as guidelines for any major or minor change that may have to be made in the future.

Office planning has come a long way since its early pioneering days. It was used first as an aid to renting—as a way to show potential tenants just how their organizations would fit into some available office space. It was an uncomplicated procedure because the office buildings of those days were uncomplicated structures. There was no air conditioning and hence no large areas of inside space. Every office and every open area had windows. The process got a little more complex when window air conditioners were introduced and stuck into buildings not designed for them. When specialists first began to work together and the architect and heating and ventilating engineers got together, environmental amenities such as air conditioning and advanced lighting systems were designed into the basic building.

Paper-handling systems, material handling, word-processing work stations, security systems, audio-visual systems, etc., each with definite impact on space use, must become part of a basic analysis of space needs because the office of tomorrow will be preplanned to include them, not merely to accommodate them.

The office of the day after tomorrow, with voice-activated "printing" machines, vision telephones, and simplified accounting with no checks or currency, is a guess not so much as to what it will be but as to when it will be and when it will begin to change the way in which we house the company.

I hope this book will help you plan the office of tomorrow, and the office of the day after tomorrow, so that it will properly house the tasks to be accomplished, provide for the operational interrelationships of the occupants, act as an information-processing machine and also, if successful, emphasize, through planning and design, that this is a place where people work.

If the book helps, I shall feel rewarded. So will a number of other people—several of my client friends who encouraged me to write this book, some of my planner and designer friends who thought this could be an important compilation of the information necessary for a planning project, some of my consultant friends, each of whom added to my knowledge in his particular field, Bill Salo, who first nurtured the idea when I spoke to him about it, Jerry Robinson, who encouraged it from the moment he read the outline, Andrew Alpern, whose enthusiastic comments made me work a little harder at it than I otherwise might have worked, Peter Pattison, who gave validity to all the sections dealing with real estate, and my wife, who, having read the manuscript too many times, refrained from throwing it at me. Instead she simplified and clarified many of my overstatements and all my stuffy attempts at erudition.

My thanks to all of them for adding more substance to this book than it would otherwise have had and for making the whole thing easier to understand and to use.

Michael Saphier

PLANNING THE NEW OFFICE

I
The Need
for Change

1 An Evaluation of Present Space

Few companies move—or redo existing quarters—because the wall in the president's office is dirty or because the chairman of the board sold a cooperative apartment in the city, moved to the suburbs, and wants to be within walking distance of the office. Tales of this sort make good business lunch conversation, but company moves are made because of legitimate needs for change.

There are four such basic needs—four reasons that make companies decide to move or redo their offices. Some are predictable far enough in advance to allow sufficient time to plan ahead, while others, the result of unpredictable events, can force the unwary into making unnecessarily rapid, and often wrong, decisions. Along with descriptions of the reasons for change and suggestions for advance charting of the predictable ones, the text includes methods for dealing calmly with the unpredictable ones.

Each change, whether it involves a move or renovation or a redecoration, must be carefully studied and cost-accounted and the advantages and disadvantages analyzed in a feasibility study before any decision is made to embark upon a "change" project, large or small. Redecoration, by way of explanation, is exactly that: a decorating again. Renovation is replanning and redecoration.

The feasibility study is a very important preliminary step. Too often companies, having established the fact that there is a need for change, jump right into the total project effort. Experience proves that much time, effort, and money can be wasted by plunging headlong into a project without preparing a basic preliminary evaluation of the goals to be reached and the dollars it must take to reach them. Such an analysis helps to chart the course a project should take and to avoid dead ends and blind alleys. The chapters in Section I outline the methods that should be taken in preparing this feasibility study.

The forms and charts suggested for use in the preparation of the feasibility study are illustrated in this section. To keep them as clear and as understandable as possible, they have been based on the needs of a small, hypothetical company, the "Adams Mail Sale Corporation." The project effort described in this book will be equally valuable to the hypothetical company, to companies ten times its size, or to companies a hundred times as large. The forms will be the same no matter what the size of the company.

As the first step in the evaluation of present space, it is advisable to have an inventory of the existing organization and the space it occupies. For those companies that have no such inventory, Figure 1-1 shows a simple, practical approach to the subject, that should be fairly easy to prepare. Later, in conjunction with the work done for an actual move, this information will become part of a permanent inventory of space and equipment and will thus be available, updated, to help in any further changes that may have to be made.

The inventory need not be any more complicated than the illustration, particularly since it will become quickly outdated if a change takes place. The prime function of this or any other inventory form that may exist is to allow the management of a company to have in front of it, during all discussion concerning the possible operational changes, a visual presentation showing the major components of the organization. If it is to be of help, the inventory of existing space should list all departments, the job categories within each of them, and the service areas. The breakdown of job categories can be as detailed as necessary for an understanding of each department. The name of each department head should be listed, as should the name of anyone else within the department who is empowered to speak for that department in operational or organizational discussions. The number of people in each job category or service area should be shown, the type of area each occupies, i.e., private office, semiprivate office, or open area, and, if possible, the square feet each occupies. The dimensions are not vitally important and should be charted only if readily available.

If the dimensions are listed, they should include private offices and/or work stations for personnel working in open areas. The footages shown on Figure 1-1 are all "usable" square feet. The difference between "usable" and "rentable" space and the way in which work station measurements are computed will be fully discussed in subsequent chapters.

The form may contain any other information that is desired by the management of the company preparing it, but the items listed should reflect the present organization and be sufficient to help evaluate the need for change.

Figure 1-1 INVENTORY OF EXISTING SPACE

The Adams Mail Sale Corporation

Date: _____

Department/Job or area category	Dept. head	No. of people	Area	Sq ft occupied*	Total sq ft for Dept.*
EXECUTIVE					1225
President	A. Adams	1	PO	300	
V.P.		1	PO	250	
Ass't. V.P.		1	PO	150	
Sec'ys.		3	OA	225	
Conf. Rm.				300	
ACCOUNTING					850
Comptroller	C. Coler	1	PO	150	
Clerks		7	OA	700	
SALES					1450
Manager	E. Edwards	1	PO	150	
Salespeople		5	PO	500	
Clerks		10	OA	800	
ADVERTISING/DIRECT MAIL					510
Manager	G. Grace	1	PO	150	
Sec'ys.		1	PO	100	
Clerks/Stenos		4	OA	260	
SERVICE AREAS					990
Conf. Rm. (Sales)				150	
Recept. Rm. (Exec.)				225	
Library (Advert.)				135	
File Room	H. Henry	1		135	
Storage/Supply		1		120	
Mail Room				100	
Photocopy/Repro.				125	
Tel. Equip.				0	
Lounge				0	
TOTAL SQUARE FEET					5025

Legend: PO—Private Office; OA—Open Area

*These figures should be entered *only* if they are readily available.

The first of the basic needs for change is *the need for more space*. This, almost without exception, is a people problem; the need for more people to run the "business machine" that is the office of today. This need for more people, and hence the need for more space, is brought about by normal business growth, "product" growth, or growth through acquisition.

The need for more space because of *normal business growth* is basically predictable and hence chartable. Even though such predictions may often be no more than "cloudy crystal ball gazing" or educated guessing, a chart showing anticipated company growth must be prepared, kept as accurately as possible, and updated frequently. There is certainly no more effective way to help determine when and if a move should be made. The growth projection worksheet, Figure 1-2, is as valid for the ten or so thousand square feet of space represented on it as it would be for any organization, no matter how large. Requirements can be charted in yearly increments as illustrated, in 2-year increments, or in 5-year increments, whichever is meaningful for the organization involved. It can also be extended for as many multiples of that increment as can be intelligently projected. This too would depend upon the nature of the organization and its growth predictability. Because projections of future needs must definitely be prepared when a move is being planned, a detailed discussion of projections, projection techniques, and methods of tabulating projections is contained in Section II, Chapter 7. The illustrated projection worksheet is shown as an example of the kind of projection chart that can be helpful in preparing the preliminary feasibility study. It was prepared for the same sales company for which Figure 1-1 was prepared, and was compiled one year after the company had moved into its space. The signed lease was for a period of ten years and for 7500 sq ft of space (usable) with an additional 2500 contiguous sq ft of space (usable) to be made available at the end of the third year should the company elect to rent them. The preparation of the worksheet was an attempt to help to determine whether or not the additional footage would be needed at the end of the third year and what the continuing space problem would be over a 10-year period. Because the company was already in the space, existing space standards were used for both personnel areas and service areas. As in Figure 1-1, the footages shown are usable square feet.

The worksheet, prepared in the second year of the company's occupancy of its space, with a number of statistical factors used as a base for quite valid projections of growth, proved that (1) by the time the additional 2500 sq ft became available, the option to obtain it would have been exercised, and (2) should the projections hold up, additional space would have to be obtained by the seventh year. If additional space is not available at that time, the company may want to try to negotiate a lease for space somewhere else and attempt to have the new landlord take on the responsibility for leasing the old space. If that cannot be done, the company may be forced to crowd personnel into existing space until the expiration of the lease makes it possible to move. Here again the worksheet provides the information necessary to work out a logical timetable of events.

Once space requirement projections have been prepared, the chart must be regularly monitored and the validity of the projections checked. If for reasons unforeseen at the time the projections were calculated, growth either accelerates or decelerates at a pace other than was anticipated, the chart must be adjusted for all subsequent years. At all times the target dates for acquiring (or relinquishing) space must remain clear.

Certain service areas are listed on Figure 1-2 but not shown as being used during the early years of occupancy. They do, however, become necessary as the company grows. The "lounge," for example, is an addition required by labor law in the city in which our hypothetical company lives. The actual legal requirement is for a lounge to be provided when the female population in an office reaches ten. Its size increases in direct proportion to the increase of females on the work force. This legal requirement can vary from city to city depending on local labor laws or union rules. Other service areas are enlarged, or added as required, to accommodate company growth. Note, too, that percentages have been added to the subtotal or usable footage in order to provide for interdepartmental and intradepartmental circulation. The total thus arrived at will be the usable square feet required. The calculation of percentages for circulation space as well as the difference between rentable and usable footage are explained later in this text and at a point in project chronology when such knowledge will be more pertinent.

The second reason for the need for more space, *"product" growth,* would be chartable only if it were anticipated at the time of chart preparation; otherwise product growth becomes a reason for chart editing. "Product" means either a new item to be manufactured, displayed, and sold, or a new kind of service or the extension of an existing service that will require the addition of new people to company staff. When such a product is about to be added, all statistical information that can affect the projections should be calculated and entered on the chart.

The third reason for more space is to accommodate *growth through acquisition.* Since the process of acquisition is normally slow and uncertain, it is rarely possible to prechart space needs for the acquired components and usually unwise to do so. In any event, acquisition should never be a cause for panic planning. Just as a move should be used as an opportunity to intelligently analyze company operation and organization in order to reap the benefits of possible increased efficiency through proper space use, so should an acquisition be used as a logical reason for a study of overall company policies. This is particularly true if a move is required because of the acquisition.

The importance of thorough planning instead of panic planning is well illustrated by the story of a chemical company which some years ago acquired five smaller, very specialized chemical companies. All six, housed in six different buildings, occupied 90,000 sq ft of space. When the companies had been officially acquired, the parent company decided that new space, 90,000 sq ft of it, should be found, rented, planned, designed, constructed, and occupied as rapidly as possible. A real estate broker was

Figure 1-2 GROWTH PROJECTION WORKSHEET

The Adams Mail Sale Corporation   Date:

Department/Job or area category	Sq ft	No. of people	Sq ft	2nd Yr		3rd Yr	
EXECUTIVE							
President	300	1	300	1	300	1	300
V.P.	250	1	250	1	250	1	250
Ass't. V.P.	150	1	150	1	150	1	150
Sec'ys.	75	3	225	3	225	3	225
Conf. Rm.	300		300		300		300
ACCOUNTING							
Comptroller	150	1	150	1	150	1	150
Clerks	100	7	700	8	800	9	900
SALES							
Manager	150	1	150	1	150	1	150
Salespeople	100	5	500	5	500	5	500
Clerks	80	10	800	12	960	13	1,040
ADVERTISING/DIRECT MAIL							
Manager	150	1	150	1	150	1	150
Sec'ys.	100	1	100	1	100	1	100
Clerks/Stenos	65	4	260	6	390	8	520
SERVICE AREAS							
Conf. Rm. (Sales)	150		150		150		150
Recept. Rm.	225		225		225		225
Library	135		135		135		135
File Room	135	1	135	1	135	1	135
Store/Supply	120	1	120	1	120	1	120
Mail Room	100		100		100		100
Photo/Repro.	125		125		125		125
Tel. Equip.							
Lounge							
TOTAL			5,025		5,415		5,725
15% Intracirculation			753		812		858
Subtotal			5,778		6,227		6,583
10% Intercirculation			578		622		659
Total usable required			6,356		6,849		7,242
Usable under lease			7,500		7,500		7,500
Add'l. usable required			0		0		0

	4th Yr		5th Yr		6th Yr		7th Yr		8th Yr		9th Yr		10th Yr
1	300	1	300	1	300	1	300	1	300	1	300	1	300
1	250	1	250	1	250	1	250	1	250	1	250	1	250
2	300	2	300	2	300	3	450	3	450	3	450	4	600
4	300	4	300	3	300	5	375	5	375	5	375	6	450
	300		300		300		300		300		300		300
1	150	1	150	1	150	1	150	1	150	1	150	1	150
9	900	9	900	10	1,000	11	1,100	11	1,100	12	1,200	12	1,200
1	150	1	150	1	150	1	150	1	150	1	150	1	150
6	600	6	600	7	700	7	700	7	700	7	700	8	800
14	1,120	15	1,200	16	1,280	18	1,440	18	1,440	20	1,600	22	1,760
1	150	1	150	1	150	1	150	1	150	1	150	1	150
1	100	1	100	1	100	1	100	1	100	1	100	1	100
10	650	12	780	13	845	20	1,300	20	1,300	22	1,430	22	1,430
	150		150		250		250		250		250		250
	225		225		225		225		225		225		225
	135		135		135		135		135		135		135
1	200	1	200	1	200	1	200	1	200	1	200	1	200
1	200	1	200	1	200	1	200	1	200	1	200	1	200
	150		150		150		150		150		150		150
	225		225		225		225		225		225		225
											100		100
											80		80
	6,555		6,765		7,110		8,050		8,050		8,520		9,005
	983		1,014		1,066		1,207		1,207		1,278		1,350
	7,538		7,779		8,176		9,257		9,257		9,798		10,355
	754		778		817		929		929		980		1,035
	8,292		8,557		8,993		10,186		10,186		10,778		11,390
	10,000		10,000		10,000		10,000		10,000		10,000		10,000
	0		0		0		186		186		778		1,390

called in, several buildings with 90,000 sq ft of space were found, and a space planner was retained to study the advantages and disadvantages of each building. It took no more than the first few questions that the space planner had to ask concerning the organization of the "new" company, to know that a move made at that time would create more problems than it would solve. The questions asked were the following: Who will occupy the executive area, and what title and responsibility will each occupant have? How do you intend to coordinate the three existing computer centers? Will there be six sales departments or fewer, and how many people will there be in the sales department(s)? How many traffic departments will there be and how many people in them or it?

These, and all the other questions yet to be asked, were impossible to answer and would remain impossible to answer until a thorough analysis had been made of the way in which the new company would be organized. The idea of a move was shelved while the company went to work, with management-consultant help, to determine how the organization would be structured in the future. Thoroughly aware of the fact that a move should not be planned until all the original questions that had been asked could be answered with assurance, the company now proceeded with caution, deliberately testing each organizational idea thoroughly before accepting or rejecting it.

It took two years, but at the end of that period the real estate broker and the space planner were called back. All the questions could now be answered. The company finally moved into new comfortable quarters of 35,000 sq ft of space. Three computer centers, which management originally thought would occupy space in the major office complex, were merged into one center and housed where the largest of the centers was already installed, in a building of its own adjacent to one of the plants. Had panic instincts prevailed at the time of merger, not only would far too much space have been rented and a consummate amount of money wasted, but the built-in inefficiencies that would have necessarily been part of such a move might well have caused irreparable harm to company growth.

If years of experience have proved anything, they have led to the inescapable conclusion that nothing attendant to a move should be done for expedient reasons. The money that can be wasted, the energy that can be applied inefficiently, the bad operational habits that can be perpetuated needlessly, and the opportunity for proper planning that can be lost make it mandatory that intelligent management avoid "making do" for panic reasons. It is far better to "waste" money at the beginning by paying rent for a few extra months in the present quarters, in order to assure very important savings in rent and operational efficiencies over the term of the new lease. This, of course, is true even when no mergers or acquisitions are involved. Too often companies, having drifted along without any growth projections to guide them, realize suddenly that the necessity to move is upon them. They then make plans to move without adequately studying their total operation. To move and not explore and take advantage of the possible efficiencies that can be part of a move is economically unsound. Sections II, III, and IV of this book deal with just such explorations, and no company should move without going through all of the steps of such a study.

THE NEED FOR A BETTER LOCATION

The second basic need for change comes from *the need for a better location.* This is usually not, by itself, the motivation behind a move. Most of the factors considered in the evaluation of a location are explored in conjunction with a company move that is already decided upon, and they will be thoroughly discussed and analyzed in subsequent chapters. However, a few such factors should be reviewed at this stage because one of them might be the reason for a move, even though space in the existing quarters is adequate. They are discussed in no specific order since each company has to make its own decisions concerning the relative importance of each.

Most of the factors against staying in a location that had at one time been chosen for the company home are evolutionary in nature, and those changes, which have taken place over the years, need never be a surprise to management. Although there is no column in the projections chart (Figure 1-2) for "location evaluation," such evaluation should certainly be considered and knowledge of the changes that may be taking place in building or neighborhood should be updated through observation.

A change in *the quality of the building* is usually the result of deterioration, although occasionally a building will be upgraded by modernization. Building quality is judged by the way in which it is maintained—is the building staff large enough for its tasks, are the heating, ventilating, and air conditioning kept in good repair, do the elevators work well, does the plumbing work, is adequate attention paid to required emergency repairs, is the lobby clean, are the elevators clean, are the windows washed, are the toilets clean, are they well supplied with tissues, towels, and soaps? All these things can have a negative or positive effect on staff and clients. They must be carefully weighed for the influence they can have on company efficiency and image.

A *shift of an industry center* could be a very strong influence on the evaluation of location. This is particularly true in larger cities where such industries as financial, toy, carpet, drapery, and fur each has its own area of activity within the city. Such industry concentration is helpful to industries that rely on the rapid dissemination and gathering of information. It is helpful, too, to customers who come to the city on annual or semiannual buying trips during the industry fairs and shows and can find all their sources of supply easily available. Any move of one or more of the leading companies in an industry out of one area and into another should be watched and judgments made about the effect this will have on total industry movement. The question of lease extension then becomes part of that judgment.

A general *deterioration of a neighborhood* is still another factor that could indicate the need for a move. Usually business-neighborhood deterioration is due to the upgrading and development of an area in another part of town, causing companies to move into the new, more prestigious part of the city or the suburbs. The consequent lowering of real estate values has a negative effect not only on specific buildings but on the surrounding shops, restaurants, hotels, etc., and on the general aspects of the area. This in turn can have a negative effect on personnel and on client reaction to a company.

Sometimes the problem is not one of deterioration but is instead caused by the fact that the original move to the neighborhood or individual building was made with no thought to company growth and no realization that a fully built-up neighborhood or a fully occupied building may not be able to accommodate a growing company or provide the service amenities that the company, its staff, and its clients require.

THE NEED FOR MORE EFFICIENT SPACE

The need for more efficiently planned space is the third of the four basic needs for change. The need for better planning with no real need for additional space is not usually a strong-enough reason to make a company move. A move would be made only if the new methods, equipment, systems, and procedures to be inaugurated would have a major impact on the amount of space required.

There are times when replanning is needed without a move—when a company living in one space for many years, with no need for more space or for a better location, must provide for needed operational changes. This is certainly not a predictable need capable of being charted on a growth projection worksheet. It is, however, a need that will have been anticipated well in advance of the day for changeover, since a major change in systems and procedures is never made as the result of a spur-of-the-moment decision.

Full advantage should be taken of this chance to replan. All the steps should be followed to prepare a feasibility study and the financial analysis that would be part of it. Once decisions have been made to proceed and the scope of the project has been defined, a thorough study should be made of the applicable elements of planning—as thorough as for a project involving a move to new quarters. To do anything less than such a total exploration and implementation would be to lose a rare planning opportunity.

THE NEED FOR BETTER-LOOKING SPACE

The need for better-looking space is the last of the basic needs for change. The look of the space is primarily the creation of staff environment, public environment, and corporate "image." Space that has been occupied for some time and has not been refurbished over the years will very often fail to reflect either the proper corporate image or provide the desired environment for the staff and the public. The need for better-looking space can, therefore, be the reason for a renovation or redecoration of existing space, but this need, like the need for better-planned space, is rarely the motivation for a move. Instead, it is usually the dividend accruing because one of the first three needs has become a must.

In the introduction to this book, mention was made of the interdependence of the talents and specialties that contribute to project planning. Nowhere is this interdependence better illustrated than in the subject of design. The creation of a work station, for example, is discussed in Chapters 6 and 7 as an operational problem. As such the work station components might be decided upon as a result of study by systems and procedures and forms specialists or even because of the recommendation of a behavioral scientist. However, no matter how it is approached, it remains, inescapably, an aesthetic design problem. The basic decisions concerning its form, finish, color, and general design should be made by the interior designer. The appearance of work stations, files, desks, and equipment is certainly as important in the creation of environment and company image as the design of the reception room or the president's office. The operational specialists and the designer must, therefore, work in close collaboration to create the work station. Because divided responsibility, with no leadership, usually accomplishes very little, this book will, wherever possible, point out the areas of these talent "overlaps." It will list the talents that may be involved so that overall responsibility for the completion of each can be assigned to one of the contributing specialists.

This interdependence of real estate, planning, and design talents adds emphasis to one of the basic points this book will continue to make in its discussion of office relocation: the success of a project will depend in large measure on the ability of the head of the project to properly coordinate all the knowledge offered by all the talents contributing to the project in the search for planning efficiency.

2 An Evaluation of Future Goals

The conclusion that there is need for change is but the first in a series of preliminary decisions to be made before any major planning effort should begin.

The feasibility study will be the end result of the preliminary analysis described in these first three chapters. First it will help to establish the fact that there is or is not a need for change. If there is such a need the study will then try to determine what the extent of that change should be, what the goals should be for the future, what the choices are for meeting those goals, and the approximate cost of each of those choices. It is only after the feasibility study has been completed that management can arrive at the decisions that will signal a halt to any further effort or a full-speed-ahead approach to one of the listed alternatives.

With no assurance, at the beginning, that the project may proceed, it would be a tremendous waste of time and money for the feasibility study to be more than a preliminary analysis of the total problem. This is true even though some of the steps taken in the preliminary study will have to be retraced when the decision is made to proceed with a renovation or a relocation. It is important to remember, therefore, that this is not an in-depth study of the changes to be made in the future. It is a first approximation of these goals, made to help decide whether or not they are physically and financially attainable.

The need for change has been determined. The next part of the study must now help to measure the extent of that change and the number of square feet required to house the new operation. To do this, there is a series of steps that have to be taken. In going through these steps it must be kept in mind that because the aim is to arrive at a tabulation of footage requirements, the preliminary exploration into company goals must be confined only to those factors that bear on space use. For example, if a new filing system is to be considered, this could have a definite effect on the number of square feet required for the files and their use. The exact number of square feet required would have to be calculated at this point. If, on the other hand, new forms are to be designed that would have no effect on the number of files or the system of filing, the change in forms would have no impact on the number of square feet and would, therefore, be listed as something to be done in the future. Only the costs for retaining the forms consultant and for supplies or equipment necessary for the consultant's work would be included in the cost analysis. A detailed study of the subject of forms would be made only after the feasibility study had been completed and the decision to proceed had been reached.

The *orientation meeting* represents the first step in the evaluation of future goals. The information gathered will help to determine the extent of the changes to be made and will aid in the preparation of the feasibility study. These management meetings are basic to the launching of any planning project. Most projects would require that two such meetings be held. The first would be of a preliminary nature, necessary for the completion of the feasibility study. The second, more properly called a design meeting, would take place after the decision had been made to go ahead with the project.

The structure of the meetings and the people who attend depends on the mix of in-house staff and outside consultant help. This is discussed in "Project Staffing" at the end of this section. Management's responsibility at these meetings is to present a clear picture of its aims for organizational and operational efficiencies, aesthetic goals, and where possible, whatever preconceived ideas it may have concerning any financial limitations for the project.

Naturally, since these meetings are of such vital importance to project results, the top executives of the company should participate. In particular those persons in top management should attend who have the greatest knowledge of the organizational and operational aspects of the company's business. Copies of the inventory of existing space would, of course, be distributed at this meeting for management's use. The company representatives would, it is hoped, be able to verbalize the design goals to be attained in any newly planned and designed space. It is mandatory that top management attend the second of the two meetings since it is at this meeting that the design tone for the project will be set. It is desirable that they attend the first meeting, but if that should prove to be impossible, the project manager should be capable of answering (or quickly getting answers to) the questions to be covered. Definitive answers, and only definitive answers, will provide the material necessary for the preparation of a conclusive feasibility study.

Because the purpose of that study is to help decide whether or not further, more detailed studies and analyses are to be made, the questions to be asked should be broad in nature. The areas to be covered in this preliminary discussion are the organizational

and operational aims, the aesthetic goals, and the additional facilities to be considered.

Minutes of this orientation meeting should be carefully recorded on a form similar to that shown in Figure 2-1A and, like the minutes taken at any decision-making meeting, they must be complete and accurate. Since they will be used for further action, in the preparation of the feasibility study, they should be carefully organized, with each subject division and each subdivision adequately titled for rapid recognition. All information is divided into the three areas to be discussed at the meeting. The discussions concerning each organizational component are listed under the appropriate area. The minutes should also show the date of the meeting, the people who attended it, and the person or persons from whom the information was taken. Completed minutes should be initialed as accurate by that person and should be signed as approved for management by an executive designated to do so.

Figure 2-1A   PRELIMINARY REQUIREMENTS FOR FUTURE SPACE

The Adams Mail Sale Corporation

MINUTES OF ORIENTATION MEETING

Attended by: Date:

Minutes by:

ORGANIZATION AND OPERATION CHANGES
Executive Area: —add 2 V.P.'s, 1 ass't. V.P., 3 secretaries.
—enlarge executive conference room.
Sales Department—will become 2 departments with one sales manager for both. One will handle wood products and the other paper products.
Paper products department—will have 3 salespeople and 8 clerks.
Wood products department—will have 6 salespeople and 15 clerks.

AESTHETIC GOALS
Executive Area—Redesign and refurbish reception room and president's office. Double size of reception room.
—Buy new furniture for additional personnel.

NEW FACILITIES
None

Approved for Management by: Date:

Organizational and operational aims would be adequately covered using the following questions as a springboard for discussion (it must be understood that this is not an attempt to project the future growth of the company; it is an attempt to arrive at the number of square feet that will be required at the date of move-in if a change is made):

1. Are any major changes in organization contemplated (or should such changes be considered) that could affect:

   • The number and/or the organization of existing departments?

   • The number of people in existing departments?

   • The number and/or the organization of existing service areas?

   • The number of people in existing service areas?

2. Are major changes in operation contemplated (or should such changes be considered) that could affect:

   • The amount of space required (plus or minus) because of new equipment?

   • The amount of space required (plus or minus) to accommodate people because of new systems and/or procedures?

A "no" to any of these questions does not necessarily mean that these changes will never be made. There is always the possiblity that the detailed study undertaken later, when the project goes ahead, might indicate the wisdom of making such changes.

A "yes" at this time to any of these questions means that the following information should be made part of the feasibility study:

1. A tabulation of square feet needed to accommodate these changes

2. A tabulation of the costs involved in obtaining and installing the new equipment required for these changes

3. The fees and other costs that might be involved should an outside consultant or consultants be required to help effectuate these changes

AESTHETIC GOALS

The second area for discussion at the orientation meeting is the *aesthetic goals* to be met. If the change is being made only because of a need for better-looking space, this would then be the only subject that would be covered at the meeting. But whether this is the sole purpose of the meeting or not, the end result has to be to reduce design decisions to the dollars and cents it will take to implement them. From that analysis, plus the tabulation of any costs that may be involved in project completion, it can be determined whether or not the project is financially feasible.

The subject of aesthetic goals will be talked about in great detail as the project progresses, particularly at the design meeting that will be held later on. It must be discussed at this point, however briefly, for any possible effect it may have on project costs. Such things as new furniture, new cabinet work, floor coverings, draperies, wall covering, paneling, and any other items of design that may be desired must be listed in the minutes, the costs later computed on a feasibility analysis form, and the end results made part of the feasibility study.

NEW FACILITIES

The third area for discussion at orientation meetings concerns the addition of *new facilities* not currently being enjoyed. Although none of them is directly involved with the operation of any business, each could contribute in its own way to personnel and business efficiencies. Thought could be given to the inclusion of such things as a barber shop or an automobile service station or any one or more of a number of other amenities that may be helpful to company personnel or its visitors. A fairly complete list of these possible additional facilities can be found in Chapter 4, and a quick check of them might be advisable. The possible cost of installation of any that may seem desirable should later be added to the preliminary financial analysis of the project.

Department head meetings represent the next step in progress toward the feasibility study that will indicate how far the project can go. These meetings should be accomplished as rapidly as possible, particularly since all the areas now touched upon will be reexamined and all the information will be restudied in far greater detail once a decision to proceed has been made. The aim is to reach conclusions concerning the future structure of the organization. The items that will be covered in the meetings are the department and service area operations, the survey of furniture, and the survey of existing space standards. Minutes of these meetings should be as carefully recorded as were those taken at the orientation meeting. A suggested form for those minutes is shown in Figure 2-1B. The information gathered will also be used later in the preparation of the feasibility study.

In meeting with department heads to discuss *department and service area operations* the questions asked will be similar to those covered at the management orientation meeting. The answers, coming directly from operating heads, will probably be more specific in nature. The basic questions, which should act as stimuli to further questions and information, should be asked before each department head has been briefed on management's thoughts concerning the department. Later on, relevant portions of the orientation meeting minutes can be reviewed with each department head. The basic questions to be asked first are the following:

Figure 2-1B   PRELIMINARY REQUIREMENTS FOR FUTURE SPACE

The Adams Mail Sale Corporation

MINUTES OF DEPARTMENT HEAD MEETINGS

DEPARTMENT: Accounting   Date:

Info. from: Charles Coler
                        Add 2 clerks,
                        Required furniture—2 desks/2 chairs/3 files.

DEPARTMENT: Sales (Paper and Wood Products)   Date:
Info. from: E. Edwards
                        New Space Standards—Salespeople and clerks to have
                                    work stations of 50 sq ft . . .
                                    —Sales Manager to now get
                                    250 sq ft office.
                                    —New work stations and files to
                                    replace existing desks and
                                    files.

DEPARTMENT: Library (used by Advertising Department)   Date:
Info. from: G. Grace
                        Add 150 square feet to Library.
                        New shelves required—refinish existing shelves to
                        match new ones.

Approved for Management by: Date:

1. Are there any major changes contemplated that could affect:

   • The number of people in the department (or service area)?

   • The amount of space required (plus or minus) because of new equipment?

   • The amount of space required (plus or minus) to accommodate people because of new equipment or new systems and procedures?

2. If people are being added, is new furniture and/or equipment needed for them? If so, what would these new items be?

3. If additional space is to be added to expand a service area, is any new furniture and/or equipment required? If so, what would these new items be?

Any further information gathered at this time should be confined to those things that will affect the amount of space to be used or the dollars to be spent.

The second item that must be covered and discussed with department heads in this study of the organization, is a *survey of existing furniture* in use. Here again this is not the complete, detailed inventory and analysis of every bit of furniture and equipment. Such an inventory has to be prepared only if a change is approved and work on the project proceeds. It is, instead, a preliminary analysis, the purpose of which is to help determine rather rapidly just how much of the existing furniture and equipment might have to be replaced or refurbished. Information and decisions concerning this reuse or replacement should come from the department heads. Management would have final approval.

The *survey of existing space standards,* next on the agenda for department head discussion, could have a very direct bearing on the acquisition of new furniture and/or the amount of square feet of space to be occupied. The whole subject of space standards is covered in detail in Chapter 7 and should be thoroughly studied at a later time in project progress. At this stage only a preliminary survey should be made and reviewed with the department heads, and any obviously advantageous space standard changes should be discussed with them. Any agreed-upon changes could then be made part of the feasibility study calculations.

An example of this kind of advantageous change is shown in the minutes of the department head meeting, Figure 2-1B. In the sales department, new standards of 50 sq ft per salesperson and per clerk are suggested to replace existing standards of 100 sq ft each. This requires new work stations and new files which would be part of the work stations, to replace existing desks, chairs, and files. Later calculations will show that an increase from twenty-three salespeople and clerks to thirty-two actually results in a 280 sq ft decrease of space required for the department. This change in space standards will entail an expenditure for the new work stations, and the cost of these stations will later be compared with the possible costs of the alternative if the new space standard is not adopted.

It would be a good idea at this point, with the orientation meeting and the department head meetings completed, to organize the information already gathered. Eventually the end result of the feasibility study will be a feasibility/financial analysis sheet that will recap all the information management will neet to help it make decisions about the project. Figure 2-2 shows a suggested worksheet form on which the information gathered to this point can be entered. Any additional information required for the feasibility analysis can also be entered on this form, as can all the calculations of project costs.

Please note that all these forms list the responsible department or service-area head

Figure 2-2 PRELIMINARY REQUIREMENTS FOR FUTURE SPACE—WORKSHEET

The Adams Mail Sale Corporation			Date:	
EXISTING			NEW	
People	Sq ft	Personnel/facilities	Add'l. sq ft	Furniture/equipment/design
8	1450	EXECUTIVE DEPARTMENT		
		2 Vice Presidents	500	2 Desks
				2 Swivel Chairs
				4 Arm Chairs
				2 Sofas
				2 Bookcases
		1 Ass't. Vice Pres.	150	1 Desk
				1 Swivel Chair
				2 Arm Chairs
		3 Secretaries	225	3 Desks
				3 Swivel Chairs
				3 Typewriters
				6 Files
		Conf. Rm./Projection		Projection Equip. including
		Rm.	150	Screen
	225	Reception Room	225	Redesign Recept. Rm.*
				Redesign President's Office*
	1675		1250	
24	2130	SALES DEPARTMENTS		
		(Wood & Paper Products)		
		2 Salespeople/7 Clerks	−(280)	32 work stations—includes
				desk, chair, files, and
				partitions
11	1150	ACCOUNTING		
		2 Clerks	200	2 Desks
				2 Chairs
				2 Files

Unit price	Total $	Total sq ft	Remarks
600.	1200.		
200.	400.		
250.	1000.		
700.	1400.		
150.	300.		
400.	400.		
100.	100.		
150.	300.		
300.	900.		
100.	300.		
650.	1950.		
150.	900.		
	10000.		
	7500.		*This includes new furniture,
	13000.		furnishings, wall treatment
	$38750.	2925	and lighting.
			Reduction in footage is because of
1800.	$57600.	1850	new space standards: Mgr's. office
			250 sq ft, Salespeople & Clerks (32)
			each 50 sq ft.
300.	800.		
100.	200.		
150.	300.		
	$ 1100.	1350	

who must either provide or else approve all the information shown. Note too that all forms that carry requests for space, personnel, furniture, equipment, or changes in procedure have a line for top management's written, signed approval. All requests that will have a bearing on organization or operation changes or on dollars to be spent should be so approved by top management before being made part of the feasibility analysis.

The first two columns of Figure 2-2 show the number of people now (sixth year, Figure 1-2) in each department and service area and the number of square feet being utilized. The next columns show information relative to new personnel, facilities, furniture, equipment, etc., which should be taken from the minutes of the orientation meeting and the department-head meetings. In addition to listing new furniture and equipment required for new personnel or procedures, listing should be made of all requested elements of design. Anticipated costs for all this must also be entered. These costs and the budgeting of these elements of design are discussed in Chapter 11.

Each department can be given its own worksheet, or one sheet can be used for several departments. This, of course, would depend upon the amount of information to be entered.

FINANCIAL GOALS

The third stage in the evaluation of future goals is the *tabulation of footages and the financial requirements*. Its purpose is to reduce to the reality of numbers the organizational and operational requirements that have been gathered. It is necessary to know how many square feet of space are required for the future and how many dollars are needed for the furniture, equipment, and talents necessary to implement those goals. Only then can all the choices available for future action be properly analyzed.

Figure 2-3 was designed to help recap the information already gathered, extend the units to totals, and add to that information the costs of the additional elements that would be needed for the completion of the project. It should also be used in the financial analysis of the choices to be explored in Chapter 3 and will finally wind up as the financial summary of the feasibility study.

The first page of the form starts with a list of the departments and service areas. Column 1 shows the square feet required by each department (from Figure 2-2) and to that total is added the percentages for inter- and intradepartmental circulation. The result is the total of usable square feet required for the company. Column 2 lists the personnel, existing and new, by department. In case the additional payroll for this new personnel is to be a factor in deciding on the changes that would be made, column 3 provides space for listing the annual payroll increase by department. Column 4 lists the dollars required by department for new furniture, equipment, and elements of design. This, too, is a recap of information from Figure 2-2.

Should there be any large single expenditure that might be subject to management question, it would be advisable to analyze other possiblities (if any exist) before presenting final conclusions. For example, the suggested change in sales department space standards, which would result in a savings of square feet, necessitates an expenditure of $57,600 for new work stations. The decision to spend the money should be made only after an analysis of what would happen if the money were not to be spent. The mathematics of such an analysis is shown in Figure 2-3.

1. Furniture would have to be provided for the nine people joining the department . . . . 9 × $550. $ 4,950.

2. There would have to be construc-tion costs for 1350 additional square feet of space . . . . 1350 × $15. $20,250.

3. There would be moving costs for 1350 additional square feet of space 1350 × $1.50 $ 2,025.

Total cash outlay . . . . $27,225.

Also, the company will be taking on an annual cost of rent for the 1350 sq ft of new space required. At the prevailing local rent of $8 per square foot, this would mean a yearly cost, plus normal rent escalation, of $10,800. All of this adds up to the inescapable fact that within 3 years the company would have spent more than the $57,600 cost of the new work stations and still be faced with an additional $10,800 annual cost for the length of the lease.

Although there are quite a number of other costs that will be involved in project completion, most of them are directly tied to decisions yet to be made about building or renting or refurbishing. Those costs will be calculated when that stage in analysis is reached.

For the moment, the only other potential costs that could be included are those for the consultant efforts necessary to effectuate the possible changes. Only those efforts that are measurable at this point can be listed. For example, while studying the operation of the sales department, it was thought that a redesign of sales forms could affect economies and efficiencies. The cost of a forms consultant and the cost for art work and plates necessary to print those forms will be the same whether the company rents, builds, or refurbishes. Although the redesign of forms will have little impact on the amount of space to be used, these costs can be calculated at this point. The cost of space-planning and/or architectural services, however, will depend on the eventual extent of the project and can be calculated later when guidelines become clearer. The consultant help available and the cost of that consulting effort are listed and described in the "Project Staffing" addendum to each section. These addenda should be used as a checklist to make certain that the costs for all possible help are included in the budget.

The in-house staff or outside consultants, to be used if the project proceeds, should now be listed on the Financial Analysis Sheet of Figure 2-3. The consultants' costs are

Figure 2-3 FEASIBILITY ANALYSIS

The Adams Mail Sale Corporation   Date:

		WORKSHEET			
DEPARTMENT	Sq ft required	Personnel Exist.	+ Req'd.	Add'l. payroll (when req'd.)	$ Req'd. for new furn. Des.
Executive	2,925	8	6		38,750.
Accounting	1,350	11	2		1,500.
Sales	1,850	24	9		57,600.[a]
Advertising	1,550	15	7		3,500.
Conference Room	250				3,000.
Library	290				3,500.
File Room	200	1			
Storage/Supply	200				
Mail	150				
Photo/Reproduction	225				
Telephone Equipment	200				
Lounge	80				
Total	9,270	59	24		$105,150.
15% Intracirculation	1,390				
Subtotal	10,660				
10% Intercirculation	1,066				
Total Usable Required	11,726				

a. This expenditure is for new work stations if new space standards are to be used.

If these new standards are not to be used and work stations are not purchased, the following costs will have to be incur

Annual rent for 1350 additional square feet @ $8.00—$10,800.

Furniture for nine people @ $550.00 per person — 4,950.

Construction for 1350 add'l. sq ft @ $15.00 — 20,250

Moving costs for 1350 add'l. sq ft @ $1.50 — 2,025.

FINANCIAL ANALYSIS: ADDITIONAL SPACE—NEW LOCATION		
CONSULTANTS AND RELATED COSTS	Rent (14,400 ▱)	Build (15,000 ▱)
Project Manager	—	—
Project Director (flat fee)	$ 15,000.	$ 15,000.**
Audio Visual (fee + equipment)	5,000.	5,000.**
Library (fee)	750.	750.**
Reproduction (fee + equipment)	1,250.	1,250.**
Forms (fee + artwork & plates)	4,500.	4,500.**
Real Estate—(B) Broker, (C) Consultant	(B)—	(C) x**
Financial	x	x**
Legal	x	x**
Space Planning/Interior Design ($1.20 ▱)	17,300.	18,000.**
Architect/Engineers (10% of cost)	—	90,000.
Construction Manager	—	x
RENT/CONSTRUCTION/PURCHASES		
Rent 14,400 sq. ft. @ $8.00*	115,200.*	—
Add'l. Furniture, Equipment & Design	105,150.	105,150.**
Interior Constr.—after work letter—$15. ▱	216,000.**	—
Moving Costs @ $1.50 ▱	21,600.	21,600.**
Telephone Installation @ $1.00 ▱	14,400.	14,400.**
Constr.—including interiors—$60. ▱	—	900,000.
Land	—	x
Investment for Building (initial)	—	x
Tax Savings	—	x
Interest, Amortization & Taxes	—	x
Operating Expenses—Bldg. Maintenance*	—	x**
Total—nonrecurring expenditures		
Total—annual operating expenses (due to move)		
Total (if applicable)—expenditure (or possible profit) for disposing of existing real estate commitments (leases or property owned)		

* Annual costs subject to escalation.

**These costs would be applicable also if the building were erected to specifications, constructed by others, and rented under a net lease arrangement.

x, Amount unknown; —, not applicable; ▱, architectural symbol for "square feet."

also shown there. The first two talents listed are fully described in the "Project Staffing" addendum to this section. The project manager is considered a company staff person, while the project director is a retained consultant.

Next on the list is an audio-visual consultant, who will design a small audio-visual aid to be used in the sales department conference room. The price shown is for consultant effort and equipment. The library consultant listed will specify and oversee the installation of a new filing and ready-reference system. No equipment is required. The reproduction area requires a change in layout plus the addition of collating equipment. The cost shown is for equipment and design. The forms-consultant effort includes the design of new forms, the art work for them, and the preparation of repro plates. Production of the forms will be done in-house, as before.

All the information now entered on the worksheet of Figure 2-3 will be common to the project, no matter which of the choices described in Chapter 3 is decided upon.

3 An Evaluation of the Choices for Meeting These Goals

With the need for change determined, and the preliminary evaluation of future goals completed, study must now be made of the various ways that are available for meeting those goals. This is the third and last step that will help to decide whether or not a change will, and can, be made.

The purpose of this study is to determine how best to house the square feet required for the operational changes. If the company contemplates a move to *new space* because more and/or better space is needed, does the company rent or build? If it builds, does it build a single-occupancy building, a multiple-occupancy building, or an extension to an existing warehouse or plant? If more space is needed and the *existing space is satisfactory,* does the company rent additional space contiguous to existing space or build additonal space contiguous to the existing space if the building is company-owned? If *no additional footage* is required, but more efficiently planned and/or better-designed space is desired, does the company renovate or redecorate the existing space?

These then are the possibilities to be considered. Although this represents quite a number of choices, only a few of them will be applicable to any given situation. Those that are must be analyzed, the pros and cons of each carefully weighed, and the total costs tabulated.

Part of that analysis must include judgments concerning present lease involvements: How long do leases have to run? Can they be terminated by the payment of a penalty and, if so, how much of a penalty? If not, can the space be subleased and at what sacrifice or profit? The answers to these questions can be quickly arrived at and must be included in the preliminary feasibility study.

The requirements of the hypothetical company, the Adams Mail Sale Corporation, have been charted on Figures 1-1 to 2-3. These needs will continue to be used until the feasibility study has been completed in order to show how each of the possibilities should be analyzed.

It is important to remember that for this feasibility analysis whatever comparisons are made must be consistent and must be computed from the same basic premise. The study done so far shows a tabulation of square feet required for an almost immediate move-in date. All rental figures, construction figures, and other project costs will be based on that square-foot number, despite the fact that if a move is made, the number of square feet that would eventually be rented or built may be far different from the number used in this exercise. The reason for this is that for the hypothetical problem no projections of future growth have been made. Such projections will be done later, after the decision to change has been finalized.

From what has been learned of the Adams Mail Sale Corporation there is no doubt that more square feet are required to accommodate the desired changes than are now under lease. On the assumption that the company wants to move into new space, the alternatives for providing that new space are either renting or building.

To keep all cost accounting closer to reality, the usable-square-feet figure should now be converted into a rentable figure. In many localities rentable and usable figures are the same (see Chapter 8). Where there is a difference, the exact conversion factor for each building under study can be calculated and supplied by the building owner or renting agent and checked for accuracy later by the consultant space planner or architect. For the preliminary feasibility, with no actual buildings yet decided upon, an average factor of 1.2 can be used. By multiplying 12,000 sq ft, usable, by 1.2, the rentable figure becomes 14,400 sq ft. For this exercise, therefore, in all rental situations being analyzed, costs based on a square-foot unit should use 14,400 as the multiplicand. The factor for a building, by the way, is arrived at by dividing the rentable footage by the usable. The rentable footage, usually supplied by the building architect or agent, is the usable area plus a proportionate share of that part of the building not directly usable as office space by tenants—space such as toilet rooms, air conditioning, electrical and telephone equipment rooms, and similar spaces. The usable footage is calculated by measuring the actual area on a floor that is available for layout.

In each of the choices to be studied the first thing to be considered should be the specialized talents that may be utilized. The reason for doing this at the beginning is that these specialists may have to be consulted and their help sought in cost accounting those parts of the project on which they might be used.

In analyzing the possibilities and tabulating their comparative costs the analysis section of Figure 2-3 will be used. For illustrative purposes, three variations of this section are shown. The first, on Figure 2-3, is for an analysis of additional space in a new location. On it are first entered those specialties earlier decided upon as being common to all alternatives. Next should be listed those specialists whose talents would be used in connection with a move to new space. It would be a good idea to list all possible help even if there may be no charge for services (such as a real estate broker) or if such services are in-house or on retainer. This would give management an opportunity to see what kind of help is needed and to decide whether or not additional outside help would be desirable.

RENT

If the company is going to rent space, help in doing so can come from the following specialists (their functions will be fully detailed in "Project Staffing" under that section in which their help is utilized; here they are listed only for inclusion in the financial analysis of the feasibility study):

1. *Real estate specialists.* For 14,400 sq ft of space a broker would be used, whose fee would be paid by the landlord of the building in which space was rented. If a greater number of square feet were involved, a real estate consultant could be used to help analyze and compare the various buildings being considered and to help negotiate the terms and conditions of the lease.

2. *Financial advisor.* Except in situations involving land acquisitions, mortgage financing, or construction financing, financial advice would usually come from within the company or from the company bank.

3. *Legal advisor.* Legal help would include advice on lease preparation and work letter details as well as aid in lease negotiations.

4. *Space planner/interior designer.* This could be handled by one company or by a space planner and an interior designer working as separate entities.

   If the move means a relocation to a totally different part of the country, it may be necessary to use both a *location consultant* and a *personnel relocation consultant.* (Both are described in "Section III: Project Staffing.") The one will help the company determine where to move, based on such things as business needs, demographic studies, and analysis of personnel availability, transportation, and taxes in the desirable locations. The other will help set personnel policies such as severance benefits for those people not moving and relocation help for those who are.

   In addition to the cost of consultant effort, the following cost factors must be tabulated:

1. *Rent.* This is an annual cost subject to escalation.

2. *New furniture, equipment, and design elements.* These costs have already been tabulated in Figure 2-3.

3. *Basic construction.* Construction costs are those in addition to the allowances given under the work letter portion of the lease.

4. *Moving costs.* If the move is a relocation of some distance, this must include the costs of moving personnel and of severance benefits for those not moving.

5. *Insurance.* For a move to only 14,400 sq ft of space the major coverage should be provided by the moving company. Any unusual items of value could be covered separately and such cost, if meaningful, should be listed.

6. *Telephone installation.*

Another choice to be considered would be to *rent additional space contiguous to existing space.* If additional space is available, this possibility can be analyzed so long as the location and the quality of the building presently housing the offices are satisfactory. The comparative analysis between renting and building as an addition to existing space is shown on Figure 3-1A, along with the additional footages required for the single- and multiple-occupancy alternatives. No additional consultants would be required other than those already discussed. The other costs would be affected as follows:

1. Rent would probably be less in an older building.

2. Construction costs could be higher because in all probability the landlord would not be as generous with work letter allowances when negotiating a new lease.

3. An amount per square foot would have to be added for the demolition work to be done to accommodate the redo of presently occupied space of 10,000 sq ft, usable, or 12,000 sq ft, rentable.

There would be no moving costs involved and the cost for telephone installation would be considerably less, unless a complete new system were to be installed. The amount listed on Figure 3-1A is for new phones for the new space.

BUILD

The company contemplating the second choice, *building* its own office building, has three possibilities open to it: a single-occupancy building, a multiple-occupancy building or an extension to an existing structure. Only the first will be explored in any detail here. The problems involved are really the same in all three possibilities. They, and whatever exceptions there are in each, will be described in Section III.

To calculate the cost factors for a single-occupancy building, it is necessary to go back to the usable square feet originally tabulated and add to it a factor of 25 percent in order to calculate the gross footage of this new building. The 25 percent factor, by the way, is a rule-of-thumb figure that can vary somewhat from one building to another. The gross footage, detailed in Chapter 8, takes into account such building elements as toilets, elevators, stairways, equipment rooms for building services, thickness of exterior

The Adams Mail Sale Corporation		Date:	

FINANCIAL ANALYSIS: ADDITIONAL SPACE, EXISTING LOCATION

CONSULTANTS AND RELATED COSTS		Rent—Add (2,400 ⌷)	Build—Add (3,000 ⌷)
Project Manager		—	—
Project Director	(flat fee)	$15,000.	$15,000.
Audio Visual	(fee + equipment)	5,000.	5,000.
Library	(fee)	750.	750.
Reproduction	(fee + equipment)	1,250.	1,250.
Forms	(fee + artwork & plates)	4,500.	4,500.
Space Planning/Interior Design ($1.20 ⌷)		17,300.	18,000.
Architect/Engineers (10% of cost)		—	18,000.
RENT/CONSTRUCTION/PURCHASE			
Rent—12,000 + 2,400 (new) @ $6.00* ⌷		86,400.*	—
Add'l. Furniture, Equipment & Design		105,150.	105,150.
Interior Construction—after work letter, @ $18 ⌷		289,200.	—
Demolition (12,000 ⌷) @ $3.00 ⌷		36,000.	36,000.
Telephone Installation—added space @ $1.00 ⌷		2,400.	3,000.
New Construction—including interiors—			
12,000 ⌷ @ $20.00 ⌷		—	240,000.
3,000 ⌷ @ $60.00 ⌷		—	180,000.
Investment for Building (initial)		—	x
Tax Savings		—	x
Interest/Amortization/Taxes		—	x
Operating Expenses—Bldg. Maintenance*		—	x
Total—nonrecurring expenditures			
Total—annual operating expenses (due to move)			

*Annual costs subject to escalation

x, Amount unknown; —, not applicable; ⌷, architectural symbol for "square feet."

walls, etc. Since the usable footage required for the hypothetical company is 12,000 sq ft, adding a 25 percent factor to it means that the gross building footage will be 15,000 sq ft. Cost calculations for those items measured by a square-foot unit should therefore use 15,000 as the multiplicand in those situations where a building is being constructed.

The outside help required in a building situation, in addition to or instead of the help already listed for a rental situation, would be:

1. *Real estate specialists.* In this case a *real estate consultant* could be used, who would, for a fee, help in locating a site, evaluate problems connected with the site selection such as transportation and personnel availability, and help negotiate for its acquisition.

2. *Financial advisor.* The building situation may require financing advice and help as far as land purchasing and mortgage financing are concerned.

3. *Insurance.* This may cover construction and structure.

4. *Construction manager.* On a large project this would be the overseer of the entire general contractor effort.

5. *General contractor*

6. *Architect/engineers*

The other cost factors, in addition to or instead of those listed for the rental situation, would be:

1. Basic building costs
2. Cost of land
3. Initial investment for building
4. Tax savings
5. Interest and amortization
6. Annual building operating costs

There is a variation on this possibility that should be considered—that of having a single-occupancy building constructed to company specifications, financed and owned by a developer. It could be rented under a net lease arrangement with rent and all operating costs paid for by the company.

The choice, *to build additional space contiguous to existing space,* would be a possibility if the building were already company-owned. The building of approximately 3000 gross square feet would be required in order to provide the required number of additional usable feet. Although building 3000 sq ft is highly unlikely as a feasible alternative, it will be followed through for the sake of showing all the steps in a complete analysis.

The Adams Mail Sale Corporation	Date:	
FINANCIAL ANALYSIS: NO ADDITIONAL SPACE		
	Renovate only	*Redecorate only*
CONSULTANTS AND RELATED COSTS		
Project Manager	—	—
Project Director	—	—
Audio Visual (fee + equipment)	$4,250.	—
Library (fee)	635.	—
Reproduction (fee + equipment)	1,060.	—
Forms (fee + artwork & plates)	3,825.	—
Space Planning/Interior Design ($1.20 ⌀)	14,400.	$6,000.
RENT/CONSTRUCTION/PURCHASE		
Add'l: Furniture, Equipment, & Design	92,450.	20,500.
Interior Construction @ $20.00 ⌀	240,000.	20,000.
Demolition @ $3.00 ⌀	36,000.	—
Telephone Installation @ $1.00 ⌀	12,000.	—
Contingent Amount for Furnishings	—	15,000.
Total		
REPAIR/REPLACE/REFINISH*		
Electrical System and Lighting	x	
Elevators	x	
HVAC	x	
Lobby and Other Public Areas	x	
Toilets and Plumbing	x	
Windows	x	
Façade	x	
Total		

*These are possible extra costs that may
be required in a modernizing program.
x, Amount unknown;
—, not applicable;
⌀, architectural symbol for "square feet."

Again the consultants would not vary to any extent from those used in the construction of a new building. The other cost factors would also be similar in nature, but not necessarily in amount. Since no work would have to be done to locate a site, a real estate specialist would not be needed and, on the assumption that there is enough land already owned to accommodate the 3,000 sq ft addition, the cost of land would not have to be included.

RENOVATE

There are two more possible solutions to the overall problem, and the analysis of each is shown in Figure 3-1B. They are predicated on the fact that, for one or more reasons, management wants no more space than is presently being occupied.

The first of these entails a *renovation of existing space.* Management would like to change as many of the operational and organizational aspects of the company as it can. They have already been discussed and tabulated, but they must now be contained in the 10,000 sq ft of usable space (12,000 rentable square feet) already under lease.

This represents a 15 percent diminution in the amount of space required to house the requested changes. Ordinarily changes like this would mean retracing footsteps and rewriting Figures 2-1 and 2-2 in order to reshape the direction and the extent of the original requirements. For this exercise it is not necessary to go that far or get that detailed, even though the end result will not be as accurate as it would have to be in an actual situation. Instead, Figure 3-1B shows that each reducible item has been cut by 15 percent and those costs, measurable as a multiple of square feet, have been edited to reflect the new, reduced amount of space. The design elements (president's office and reception room) have been left intact. The cost of all other additional furniture and equipment has been reduced by 15 percent. The project director could be eliminated in this and the next alternative, and his or her work done by in-house talent or the space planner/designer.

REDECORATE

The last choice is to *redecorate the existing space.* Management in this instance wants to make no organizational or operational changes, rent no additional space, and confine expenditures to face-lifting only. As shown in Figure 3-1B, no operational or organizational change costs are listed, no personnel added, and with the exception of some specific areas, no new furniture or equipment will be purchased.

The following suggestions for a redecorating effort will be budgeted in the financial analysis:

1. Paint the premises.

2. Refurbish the president's office and the reception room.

3. Project a dollar amount for new draperies and floor covering where needed and for any required furnishings such as wastebaskets, ashtrays, etc.

For both renovation and redecoration there are some possible extra costs that may have to be considered, particularly if the company is already in a building of its own. To modernize the building sufficiently so that the company can utilize it for an extended period, it may be necessary to repair the electrical system, the heating, ventilating and air conditioning, the elevators, and the windows and refurbish the lobby and the building façade. If so, these costs must be part of the financial analysis.

All the information has now been gathered that will enable management to judge the necessity for change, weigh the advantages to be gained by it, consider the alternatives for housing that change, and analyze the financial demands for implementing it. One other bit of information should go to management with the feasibility results and recommendations, and that is a schedule of target dates for the phased completion of the project.

How the information, which makes up the final feasibility study, will be presented to management is a decision for the project manager to make. It can be put together as a prose report backed up by the documentation of the forms prepared as part of the Section I effort, or it can be a presentation of just the forms. The method of presentation really depends upon the size of the project and on the number of people to whom the presentation has to be made. It depends, too, on the formality or informality of the presentation meeting. There is a distinct advantage to verbal presentation augmented by copies of the presentation document(s) or by slides of them. Decisions are more easily made and more easily understood when the interchange is accomplished through face-to-face dialogue. Written comment and written rebuttal can get too unwieldy, and too much of the "feel" for the company and the information gathered can be lost.

Section I: Project Staffing

The "Project Staffing" addendum that follows each section of this book contains detailed descriptions of the work to be done by both the in-house and the retained staff. Each category of effort, each talent, and/or each specialty will be discussed at the end of the section in which that effort first becomes a part of the project. In it will be described the total work that might be expected from each specialist. Whether that talent is used in whole or in part will depend upon the knowledge and abilities of the project manager and the project director.

The costs or fee arrangements for each described talent are briefly outlined, where applicable. There are a variety of ways to determine fees. The least satisfactory would be to have the consultant paid a commission, a percentage of costs, or a percentage of savings. It is important that the consultant always act in the interest of the client. To avoid any possible conflict, the consultant's fee should be a negotiated, fixed sum, or it should be based on charges for time spent on the job. The only exceptions would be the architect's fee and, in some instances, the fee of the interior designer. Also, the consultant should never be a participant in the project, i.e., one whose payment for services would come from the sale of a product. As an independent advisor, a consultant should be paid because of his or her knowledge and experience.

Nowhere in the book has any attempt been made to assign responsibilities either to staff or consultants for any specific project effort. However, the compilation and completion of the feasibility study, and the steps that lead to it as detailed in Section I, should be performed by the project manager, if he or she has the experience to do it alone, or by the project manager with project-director assistance. These two, acting in a combined role, represent the key to a successful project. "Project Staffing" describes these two roles, the talents of the people who fill them, and all the other specialties that will be required to bring the project to a successful conclusion.

In case the company does not know any specialists in a particular field, the description of each specialty is followed by a listing of some of the possible sources that would help to find the required talent. Other sources can be found in the "For Your Information" list at the end of the text.

PROJECT MANAGER

The goal of any planning project is the creation of a better business home. It is imperative that company management be aware at all times that responsibility for the project rests squarely on its shoulders. There is no valid buck passing. Success or failure is completely dependent upon management input and management guidance. Experienced space planners, architects, interior designers, and other specialists can do much to help. Their selection must be carefully considered. But of paramount importance is the selection of those people who will be part of the company staff and the person who will head that staff.

The project manager will be management's representative as decision maker and decision gatherer. The post can be filled by the office manager, the administrative officer, the executive vice president, or the president, depending upon the size of the company and the scope of the project. The project manager might be an individual working alone or with a sizable staff. In any event, he or she will be the head of the project within the company and the liason between the company and its outside consultants.

The project manager must have total knowledge of the company, its people, its organization and its operation. He or she must know how and from whom to get responsible answers quickly. With some help from a planner (or with some previous exposure to planning), a project manager could conceivably do all the work described in Section I and, without outside help, complete the feasibility study for management.

The feasibility study will define the scope of the work to be done. When management has seen it and approved the project, the defined tasks can then be assigned to company staff and such outside specialists as will have to be retained to assist. The project manager should be able to assign those tasks, decide on the staff size and talents needed, decide on the consultants required, and select or help in the selection of those who will comprise project personnel.

Experience should certainly be taken into consideration when choosing a consultant, whether it be an individual or a company. However, most projects will take from 1 to 5 years to complete. That means that other elements must also be weighed in deciding upon a consultant, including enthusiasm for the project and its importance to the consultant's own growth. But with credentials and fee all approximately the same, a major determining factor should be the "personality" of the consultant and his or her group. They all must "wear well" over the time it takes to complete the project.

The project manager must be able to administer the staff, assign individual responsibilities, and coordinate staff effort with those of the retained consultants. He or she must organize the recommendations made and be able to present them in broad, but clear, outline. When decisions are to be made the project manager must see to it that management has the opportunity to examine intelligent choices.

PROJECT DIRECTOR

This is a special talent filling a new need that has recently evolved in space-planning projects. Tried in only a few instances up to the time of this writing, it is, nevertheless, a talent whose value daily becomes more and more apparent. One day, soon, the project director as here defined will be the accepted and welcome leader of all planning and design tasks.

In the introduction to this book, mention was made of the problems management has when trying to make decisions without experience in the areas about which decisions are to be made. Couple with that the increasing number of specialists that have become participants in each planning project and the reason for the emergence of the project director becomes obvious. Someone with total knowledge of planning, from the inception to the move-in and the completion, must now sit on management's side of the table to help make the decisions.

It is this project-director effort, handled by someone who has been exposed to and experienced in all aspects of planning, that can supply the coordinating talent so necessary for project success in these days when there are so many, so varied, and such overlapping specialties. The project director should be an independent entity—not part of any group participating in any aspect of the project. There are space planners, architects, interior designers, and even some construction people who would qualify for this role, but they should be either unattached, with no company affiliations, or retained as consultants only if their companies are not hired as project participants. With nothing at all to sell except an overall knowledge of every aspect of space planning, the project director is in a unique position as project advisor to management. He or she not only is as anxious as management to complete the most efficient, most aesthetically correct planning job at the smallest possible cost, but also brings to the project the knowledge and the experience to accomplish those ends.

Another important reason for using the overview of the project director is that in each specialist's field (communications, word processing, audio-visual communications, etc.) there are dozens of salespeople, each able to make a great case for the product being sold. It takes more than just a little exposure to all the problems that must be solved to help choose the systems and equipment that will serve the best interests of the client, despite persuasive salespeople.

The project director's most difficult job, and the one most rewarding to the client if successfully accomplished, will be to turn potential conflict into cooperation. It is the project director who must see to it that the architect and the designer work together, and enjoy it! It is the project director who must see to it that the construction manager and the designer work together—that design is kept intact while the construction manager helps to save as much money as possible.

The project director could be involved in any size project, but practically, this involvement makes real sense only when the job is in excess of 50,000 sq ft of space. For jobs smaller than that, either the space-planning firm, the interior designer, or the architectural firm, with the help of the project manager, can do a coordinating job and keep management abreast of the costs, schedules, problems, and decisions. Should management, even on a smaller job, still feel the need for an independent advisor, a project director could be retained on a limited basis to help only with the feasibility study and/or to sit in on important decision-making meetings.

Whether a project director is called upon early in project chronology to help prepare the feasibility study would be a management decision and should be based upon the capabilities of the in-house project manager. On a sizable job it would be wise to bring experience to the project as early as possible. In any event the project director could be hired for only the feasibility study or for limited consultant effort on a per-diem basis on projects under 50,000 sq ft. The per-diem rate for such talent should run approximately $500 to $750 plus out-of-pocket expenses. On large projects of 50,000 sq ft or more, a flat-fee arrangement should be made with the project director. On these projects, the project director should be obliged by contract to work closely with the project manager to set up the scope of the project, list the outside consultants to be retained, aid and advise in their selection, assign task responsibilities, coordinate all project effort, approve all payments, and follow through to completion all aspects of construction, installation, and move-in.

When a project director is to be hired, two major criteria should be used in making the choice. The first must be his or her experience, and that should be extensive. The second should be the ability of company people to get along with the project director and respect his or her viewpoints. There are no short-term projects, none, that is, in which a project director would be involved. Company and consultant will be living together for quite a while, and they must be able to work together in as unabrasive a relationship as possible.

Possible sources for project director talent include:

American Institute of Architects
1735 New York Avenue N.W.
Washington, D.C. 20006

American Management Association
135 West 50th Street
New York, New York 10020

American Society of Interior Designers
730 Fifth Avenue
New York, New York 10019

Contract
1515 Broadway
New York, New York 10036

Institute of Business Designers
1350 Avenue of the Americas
New York, New York 10019

Interiors
1 Astor Plaza
New York, New York 10036

FINANCIAL ADVISOR

For the feasibility study aspect of the project, the financial advisor will probably be the company finance officer, the comptroller, the head of the accounting department, or the company accountant. The financial advisor's knowledge and experience will be used to determine how to analyze the financial involvements of buying land and building for single or multiple occupancy, and, of course, to help make the final decisions concerning the financial feasibility of the project.

Additional Effort

This help, described fully in later sections, might be needed at this time for information only:

- *Real estate specialists*—cost advice on rents, land, and existing lease involvements
- *General contractor (or construction manager)*—general advice on construction costs

There are other specialists whose knowledge might be needed for the preparation of the financial analysis of the feasibility study. Such specialists, all of whom are listed in the "Project Staffing" sections which follow, will help supply cost information on their services, on the equipment they believe may be used, and on the cost of its installation.

II
Planning for That Need

4 Planning the Departments and Service Areas

Now that the need for change has been established and the ability to make that change has been determined, the real excitement of planning for the future begins. An office move or planning change means improvement—improvement in environment, in operational and organizational efficiencies and, it is hoped, in monetary savings. How much or how little improvement will depend upon the amount and the quality of the planning effort expended by both management and its consultants, and upon the way in which that effort is organized and controlled.

ORGANIZING THE PROJECT

The need to organize the project and control each step along the way to its completion cannot be emphasized often enough or strongly enough. "Control" is the one overriding element necessary for project success. The illustrated charts or checklists are suggested methods for project control. They are but means to an end—aids to planning and controlling the work to be done, the people who will do the work, and the time schedule under which it should be done. The charts do not do the job. No Critical Path Method (CPM) or Progress Evaluation and Review Technique (PERT) chart has ever completed a project. People run projects. People prepare the control charts, assign the tasks, schedule the work, monitor the progress, adjust to the inevitable changes that take place as the project continues and, most important of all, make the decisions that keep the project moving. The control charts should indicate what has to be done, show assignments of personnel to each task, and make it possible to monitor the work to be done and the time it should take to accomplish the work. If the schedule cannot be followed, the charts should clearly indicate that fact and show the need for changes and adjustments far enough in advance to assure smooth project completion. Although some of the things to be done were covered in a preliminary way in the preparation of the feasibility analysis, the control charts should schedule those items which are to be studied in far greater detail.

In order to put the total project in proper perspective, the first step should be to map out a broad overview of all the work to be done. With the phases of effort thus established and the necessary staffing for this effort outlined, the details of project control can then be charted, phase by phase. Figure 4-1 shows just such an overview of a project. The Relocation Action List (see Appendix 1) should be used when preparing this Project Overview Chart, the Project Control Chart (Figure 4-2), and the Project Time Schedule (Figure 4-3). To avoid confusion and to simplify understanding of the phases to be followed, the organizational changes are separated from the physical changes involving real estate and building. In actuality this separation is not that complete. For example, phase III (exploring real estate alternatives) cannot be finalized until information from the survey of the future organization (phase II) has been supplied. From then on, coordination has to be constant and the recommendations must be made jointly by real estate and planners. Management, in turn, can then make the decisions required of it along the way to project completion.

Detailed project control charts will be developed to conform as closely as possible to the chronological sequence of events that should be followed. The listed staff talents will be described in detail as each of the phases of project effort is discussed.

Because much of what has to be covered in phase I was already studied in preliminary fashion when the feasibility study was prepared, the first project control chart can combine phases I and II. There should be no great problem in restudying the existing organization while at the same time surveying the elements that will, it is hoped, be part of the future of the organization. (Figure 4-2, it will be seen, is a detailed control chart for the combined phases I, II, and III.)

When the project manager/project director team (which shall be referred to only as the project manager from here on) is satisfied with this first control chart, there are a few things they must do before beginning the actual study of departments, service areas, and company operations. First they must review the corporate objectives as they were stated in the first orientation meeting, to make certain that what is done is in accordance with those objectives. (The second orientation meeting is scheduled to take place toward the end of phase II.) Then, when the kind of data to be collected has been listed on the chart, they must make decisions about who will collect the data and from whom it can be collected—in other words, who can best ask the questions and who is best equipped to give the answers to those questions. If outside help is to be brought in for data

Figure 4-1 PROJECT OVERVIEW

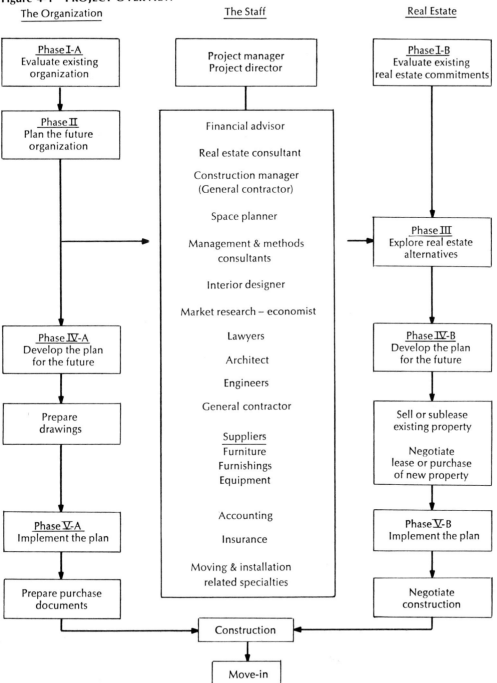

The Organization   The Staff   Real Estate

Phase I-A
Evaluate existing organization

Phase II
Plan the future organization

Project manager
Project director

Financial advisor

Real estate consultant

Construction manager
(General contractor)

Space planner

Management & methods consultants

Interior designer

Market research – economist

Lawyers

Architect

Engineers

General contractor

Suppliers
Furniture
Furnishings
Equipment

Accounting

Insurance

Moving & installation
related specialties

Phase I-B
Evaluate existing real estate commitments

Phase III
Explore real estate alternatives

Phase IV-A
Develop the plan for the future

Prepare drawings

Phase V-A
Implement the plan

Prepare purchase documents

Phase IV-B
Develop the plan for the future

Sell or sublease existing property

Negotiate lease or purchase of new property

Phase V-B
Implement the plan

Negotiate construction

Construction

Move-in

Figure 4-2   PROJECT CONTROL CHART FOR PHASES I, II, AND III

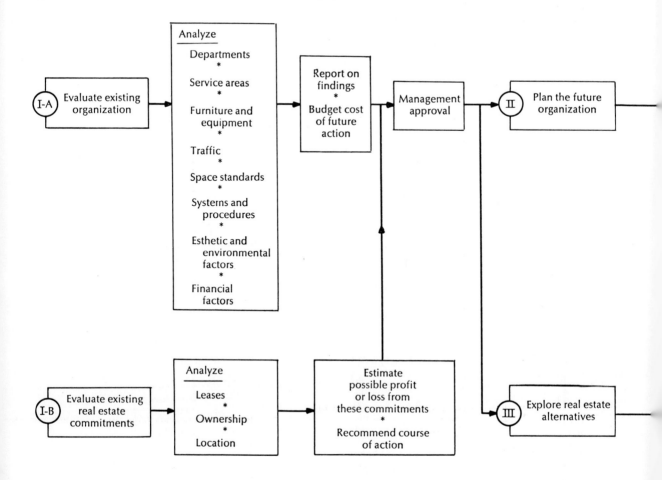

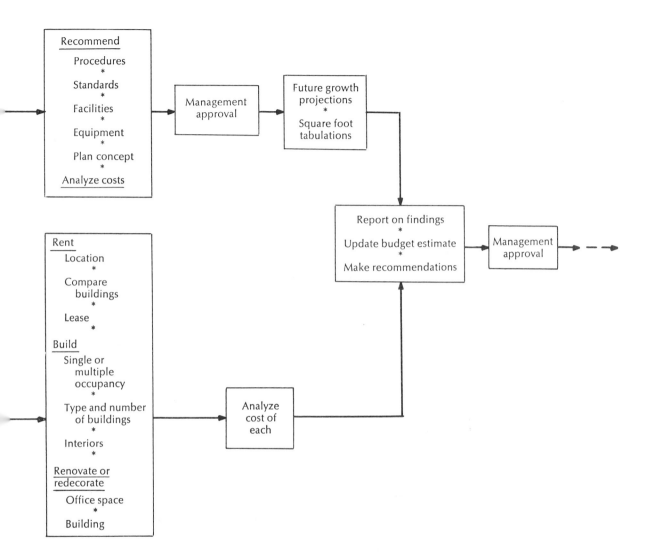

collection, or if staff people are used, they should be identified and made part of the project team now.

This is a particularly good time for management to make a decision about how space planning should be handled after the move to new quarters has been completed. If outside help will always be used, no further action need be taken at this stage. If, on the other hand, day-to-day changes are anticipated after the move-in and in-house space planning using one or more staff persons is indicated, that space-planning "staff" should become involved at this point. They should work as closely as possible with the retained space planner throughout the project, learning all they can about the reasons and the philosophy behind the space standards and the plan "concept" of space use. What they do after the move will then be in keeping with all the planning done for the move.

Large projects will require large staffs to run them. Much of the information used for making decisions will come to the project manager secondhand and to management thirdhand. It is, therefore, of vital importance that in-house staff and outside consultants and their staffs be alerted to the importance of taking detailed, voluminous notes at all meetings. Minutes and reports made from these notes should be clear and complete. These will include reports of the department head interviews, the orientation meetings, and minutes of decision-making meetings of all kinds (even phone meetings) held with anybody connected with the project.

Also, along each step of the way, arrangements must be made for the proper distribution of memos, reports, minutes of meetings, plans, specifications, invitations to bid, purchase orders, etc. It should be up to the project manager to determine who will get copies of each kind of document. Control and monitoring of the routine of distribution can be left in the hands of an assistant to the project manager, but keeping abreast of what each document contains is definitely the project manager's responsibility.

Tasks must be assigned at this time and a schedule set for this first phase. The schedule (see Figure 4-3) should be prepared with the help of those staff and consultant people who will be responsible for the timely completion of the work. Members of the project team unfamiliar with the company should be taken on a tour of all occupied space. All required forms and questionnaires that will be of help in data collection should be prepared. Examples of these forms and questionnaires will be shown, described, and discussed as each becomes pertinent to the text.

The next step should be the indoctrination of company personnel concerning the project. Some companies are hesitant about announcing too much too early. Announcements should be withheld only if management is in doubt about the move ever taking place. Otherwise experience has shown that an informed staff cooperates more completely with those involved in moving the project forward. A staff that is not told about what is going on gets nervous, apprehensive, and suspicious of the delving "strangers."

How the announcement is made is something to which management must give serious thought. A project that will take several or more years to complete should be

Figure 4-3 PROJECT TIME SCHEDULE

PHASE	ACTIVITY	ASSIGNED TO	Mar.	Apr.	May	Jun.	Jul.	Aug.	Sep.	Oct.	Nov.	Dec.
I-A	Tour Space—Prepare Forms	Staff Consult. (a)	▨									
I-A	Indoctrination Meeting	Staff Consult. (a)		▨								
I-B	Evaluate Existing Real Estate	Staff Consult. (b)	▨	▨								
I-A	Inventory Furn. and Equipment	Consult. (a)			▨							
I-A	Interview Dept. Heads	Consult. (a)				▨						
I-A	Review Systems and Procedures	Consult. (c)					▨					
I-A	Review Space Standards	Consult. (a)						▨				
I-A, I-B	Review Findings to Date	Staff/Consult. (a), (b), & (c)							▨			
I-A, I-B	Prepare Preliminary Report	Staff/Consult. (a), (b), & (c)								▨		
I	Management Approval	Staff/Consult. (a), (b), & (c)									▨	
II	Study New Procedures	Consult. (c)										▨

LEGEND:

Scheduled ▨▨

Actual ◿◿

Completed ▧▧

Consultants:

(a) Planner

(b) Real Estate

(c) Management methods, etc.

understated at the beginning, with more and more details that will evoke enthusiasm revealed as the project gets closer to the move-in date. When Sears Roebuck planned to build and move into what is the tallest building in the world, the company instituted a series of brochures that were periodically distributed to its personnel. Each brochure was designed to tell the Sears' people about another aspect of the project or another way in which their new home was planned to help individuals do their jobs and make them more comfortable in the process. One brochure dealt with the way in which the building facilities would be maintained, another told about the innovative telephone and intercom systems, another described the planning process and showed where each department would be located, while still another described the furniture that would be used and the lounge facilities that would be available. Some companies arrange to take their people on a tour of the new quarters prior to move-in. Others have prepared maps of the area around the new home and pinpointed the location of restaurants, stores, theaters, and other amenities in which the staff might be interested.

A major problem arises when the company move involves relocation to another city, with the probable severance of some employees and the required move of entire families to an unfamiliar location. This calls for very special "public relations" handling. An announcement of this kind should contain as much detailed information as possible about the personal way in which each individual problem will be treated. But disruptive though it may be, once the decision to move has been made and the details of personnel handling resolved, the announcement should be made promptly. Rumors are usually more disruptive than the truth. Public relations and personnel relocation are subjects dealt with at length in Chapter 14.

No matter how the whole subject of announcement(s) is handled, staff indoctrination must accomplish one very important thing immediately: letting company personnel know what all those people wandering around with tape measures and notebooks are really doing. Also, those company people who are expected to supply answers must be alerted to the fact that questions will be asked of them and that they must be prepared to answer them. When possible, questionnaires should be given out far in advance so that the information required can be gathered in anticipation of the interviewer's arrival. Questionnaires can be given to the people to be interviewed along with a letter of explanation, or they can be handed out at a "kick-off" meeting at which the whole subject of inventories, interviews, and the aims and hopes for the project itself can be explained by the project manager. Again, depending upon the company and the kind of project about to be started, this meeting can be a lecture only or a lecture followed by questions and answers.

FURNITURE AND EQUIPMENT INVENTORY

The first exposure that company personnel will have to the project will come when the inventory of furniture and equipment is started. It is the first step to be taken in learning about and understanding the work done in each department and service area. Like all the steps in project progress, taking the inventory will be simpler to do and easier to accomplish if it is carefully organized at the outset. The information shown on the inventory form will help to clarify departmental activity and will be vitally important in the preparation of an eventual purchasing program and, possibly, in the later development of furniture plans.

The inventory can be taken by in-house staff or by the retained space planner and his or her people. The job itself is routine, but it does require accuracy. Although it will be used as reference during the interviews that follow, it is not necessary for any of the principals of either the company or the planning consultant group to participate in taking the inventory. The planner and any key people should have walked through all of the company space prior to conducting the introductory "kickoff" meeting, the inventory, or the interviews. An overview of this kind is essential. Without it the planner can have no feel for the total company.

Preparation for taking inventory should start with the design of an inventory form unless the space-planning consultant already has a form that can be used. Figure 4-4A shows the kind of inventory form that would be quite adequate for a smaller job and could also be a worksheet for tabulating furniture or equipment changes. If the project involves a good deal of space (over 50,000 sq ft), taking an inventory will be made easier if plans of the space are made available. Each office and area can be numbered, the inventory sheet keyed to those numbers, and the two together will be a check on the accuracy of the inventory. Additionally if all, or even some, of the furniture is to be moved to the new quarters, the numbered plans will be of great help to the movers.

A very large project (several hundred thousand square feet or more) probably indicates that a certain amount of furniture standardization has occurred during the years of the company's existence. Although standardization might not be total, it is quite likely that there will be several styles of desks, chairs, files, and cabinets. If so, these styles can be coded for ease of inventory, with each team of inventory takers supplied with code sheets. For example, desks can be coded by type, style, size, and condition. The same kind of coding can be used for all other standard items. Drawings, or even photographs can be used on the code sheets in order to simplify recognition while taking the inventory.

When codes are used, untrained personnel can take the inventory, noting only those pieces of furniture and equipment that have been coded. If a team sees something that is not standard, it can flag that fact on the inventory sheet of the room or area. The flag will be noted at the end of the day by the person in charge of the inventory, who, on the following day, can send trained personnel to the area in question to make descriptive notes and take dimensions of the odd pieces of furniture or equipment.

Understand that at this point the interest in inventory should be centered around space-taking furniture and equipment and whatever office "appliances" are being used on that furniture requiring connection with a power source. Fountain pens, desk pads, and "in" and "out" baskets that sit on desks should not be part of this inventory. Telephones should be and so should electric typewriters or any other desk-top equipment requiring electricity. Figure 4-4B illustrates an inventory form for large jobs where furniture and equipment is coded to facilitate taking the inventory. This, like Figure 4-4A, can also be used as a worksheet to tabulate recommended changes.

If the inventory is an extensive one and if there is to be little replacement of either furniture or equipment, it might make sense to plan to computerize the inventory. In that case, thought should be given to the design of the form so that it includes information that might be of future use. Certainly if there is an eventual plan to buy new furniture,

Figure 4-4A INVENTORY OF FURNITURE AND EQUIPMENT

Sheet: of:

DEPARTMENT: DATE:

| I.D. No. | PERSONNEL | | EXISTING | | | | | | | | | | PROPOSED | | | | |
	Title	Name	Space	Item	Qty.	SIZE W	SIZE D	Cond.	Tel.	Elec.	Sq ft	Loc. near	Space	Item	Qty.	Sq ft

Page Total

INSTRUCTIONS: In the first column enter the identifying number of each person. This could be assigned from the personnel records and may be either a company or a department number. After entering the title and name of the person whose equipment is being inventoried, enter in the next column the kind of space being occupied (see CODE below). Space-taking items of furniture or equipment, the quantity, size, and condition of each, would then be entered in the following columns. If the occupant has a telephone, this would be listed next followed by a listing of any equipment (typewriter, adding machine, etc.) requiring electricity. The last column under "EXISTING" should show the square feet presently assigned to the individual and his equipment.

Under "PROPOSED," use identifying numbers in the "Locate near" column to indicate the desired proximity location of each person in relation to others in the department. The next columns should list recommended changes in the type of space to be occupied, the equipment to be used, and the square feet required to house all of it.

This form, edited for each specific project, could be used on jobs under 200,000 sq ft. For larger projects, the form shown on Fig. 4-4B may be more efficient.

CODE: Space:

PO —Pvt. Office
PO/2 —Pvt. Off./2 people
BSO/3 —Bankscreen Off./3 people
OA/8 —Open Area/8 people

Item:

Desk:
DP —Double Pedestal
SP —Single Pedestal
L —"L" Shaped

Chairs:
ES —Exec. Swivel
P —Posture
AS —Arm/Swivel
A —Arm

Files:
5 Lat. —5 Drawer Lateral
4 Leg. —4 Dr. Legal
4 L —4 Dr. Letter

Cond.:
G—Good
P—Poor

Elec.:
T—Typewriter
C—Calculator

Figure 4-4B   INVENTORY OF FURNITURE AND EQUIPMENT

DEPARTMENT: _____

TITLE: _____   IDENT.NO(S).: _____

ROOM OR AREA NO.: _____

DATE: _____

EXISTING											PROPOSED			
Furniture and equipment														
Space	Item	Type	Size	Cond.	Qty.	Tel.	Elec.	Sq ft	Remarks	Loc. near	Space	Item	Qty.	Sq ft

Page Total

INSTRUCTIONS: This form, which should be used only on projects of 200,000 sq ft or more, will be extremely efficient if there are large quantities of desks, chairs, files, etc., in one or more style "groups."

Before taking the inventory, plans of the existing space should be updated and numbers assigned to each room or area. Each inventory sheet would be used for one person in a private office or for a number of people, in open area, with the same job title. The kind of space would be indicated in the first column. The various styles, photographed or drawn on "code" sheets, can be letter or number coded for item (desk, chair, file, etc.) type (manufacturer and/or style), and size (where applicable, such as desk, table, file, etc.). The condition (good or poor) can be checked by the inventorior who will also enter the quantity of each, the need for telephones and list the electrical equipment in use.

The existing square feet would be taken from the plans. The "Remarks" column would be used to call attention to any odd or unusual furniture or equipment that was not coded and that should be separately inventoried.

The "PROPOSED" columns would be used as they were on Fig. 4-4A.

57

the inventory of new furniture and equipment should be put in the computer. From then on it would be a very simple matter to find out where a particular piece of furniture is located and what furniture and equipment are located in a specific building, on a floor, in a department, etc. The kind of information that can be coded for a permanent, computer-stored inventory is shown in Figure 11-5, and is further described there in connection with the purchase of new furniture.

DEPARTMENT HEAD INTERVIEWS

Interviewing each department and service area head can begin once the interviewer is armed with a complete inventory of that particular department's furniture and equipment. The inventory should be referred to during the interviewing. It should be used to check discrepancies, and it may stimulate further questions about the department.

The form of the questionnaire is relatively unimportant. It can, in fact, be nothing more than a typewritten checklist from which the interviewer asks questions. On the other hand, if the decision is to put the questions in the hands of the department heads some days before the interview takes place, the questionnaire will have to be so designed as to provide some space for writing. The person being interviewed will be expected to jot down, in advance, some of the facts needed to answer the questions.

It is important to remember that all interviews should be conducted on a face-to-face basis. Written answers will not suffice. Too many facts get lost in the shortcuts taken when writing. Also, face-to-face confrontation usually develops new areas of questions and answers that may not have been included on questionnaires, no matter how intelligently planned. One other thing should be avoided, and that is the use of tape-recording equipment when interviewing. For many reasons people tend to "freeze up" in front of a microphone or, conversely, talk too much. In either case the results are never very satisfactory and certainly not nearly so productive as the person-to-person method of gathering information.

The interviewing staff should be as small as possible, i.e., there should be as few interviewing teams as possible so that a tight rein is kept on all the information gathered. The major interviews should be conducted by the space planner in charge of the project. If another team (or teams) is required, the space planners will assign an assistant to head it. The project manager or the manager's appointed representative(s) should be present at all interviews. The minutes of these interviews (and they should be very complete and detailed minutes) should be made part of the general project file. In addition to being distributed to the project manager and the space planner, the interior designer should get a complete set of all minutes, the person interviewed should get a copy of the minutes of his or her interview, consultants should get copies of items that would be helpful to them, and a complete set should be available for management's review.

Although each situation may require some specific questions not included here, the following general questions would probably be asked in all departments:

1. Describe the function of your unit and the working relationships of its components.

2. Describe the working relationships of your department with other departments and service areas, and in order of importance, indicate those which should be located closest to yours.

2a. Is the communication with others accomplished by:

    *   Physical contact?
    *   Document delivery?

3. Do you have visitors from outside the company? If yes, how many each day? Do they need any special accommodations or facilities? Describe.

4. What are your conference room requirements? Describe the kind of facilities needed, the type of meetings held, the frequency of meetings, and the number of people who attend.

5. Do your people work overtime:

    *   At night?
    *   On weekends?

    If yes in either case, how much overtime work do they do and is it confined to any particular time of the year?

6. Are there any company security regulations for your department? Are there any government security regulations?

7. What is your secretarial policy?

    *   Private secretaries?
    *   Pooled secretaries?
    *   Other?

8. What is your record storage policy?

    *   Type of records?
    *   Type of storage?
    *   Number of storage units by type?
    *   Annual growth?
    *   Annual retirement of records?
    *   Any changes contemplated for record policy?

9. Within your department do you have your own reproduction equipment?

    *   What kind?
    *   What use does it get?
    *   Do you contemplate any changes in kind or use?

10. Within your department do you have your own library, laboratory or laboratories, data processing equipment, or any other kind of "service"? If so, please describe. Is there any special equipment used in connection with these special areas or for other purposes? If so, describe. Do you contemplate getting any other equipment?

11. Do you anticipate any major changes, either organizational or operational, in your department?

12. Are there any physical changes you would like to see accomplished in the planning of your new quarters?

13. To provide full information concerning your department personnel, please print or type the information called for on the attached sheet (Figure 4-6). Use as many sheets as you need. If there are subdivisions within your department, use separate sheets for each subdivision. Please identify each carefully. Everybody in your department must be accounted for—this includes you, your secretary, your assistant, etc. In the columns under "Proposed Number," show the number of people you anticipate having in the department by each of the indicated years.

An organization chart showing the flow of command and the flow of paper among the people in the department will help considerably in an understanding of the working relationship asked for in question 1. To augment such a chart (in place of it if one is not forthcoming) the "Locate Near" column of Figures 4-4A or 4-4B (Inventory of Furniture and Equipment) should be filled in. This will show proximity needs as dictated by usage.

The answers to question 2 will help determine the location of each department and service area within the total space to be used to house the company. It will, therefore, have a great bearing on the efficiency of the layout. One part of the question calls for a department head's evaluation of his or her department's proximity requirements. The results of such an evaluation are usually quite valid, but in actual tests, they have proven to be in error often enough to suggest more objective checking before accepting the conclusions as a reason for final layout. Department heads, although aware of the number of times they visit other departments, may be totally unaware of the traffic patterns the people in their departments actually follow, either for personal contact or for document delivery. A more objective study could bear out a department head's contention, could prove it wrong (and show the reason), or could radically alter the preconceived proximity need by showing how much more efficient a sophisticated paper-handling system and/or an improved communication system could be.

There are a number of ways such a traffic study can be made. All require the cooperation of the department's personnel. One method is to give each person a form on which he or she will tabulate whatever visits are made to other departments for conversation (other than personal) or document delivery. The results can then be calculated at the end of a given time period, which, in any event, should not be less than two weeks. Another way is to take two computer cards, each of a different color, using one for personnel visits and the other for document delivery. Each should be coded with an identifying number for the originating department. The people going from one department to another on a business visit or document delivery can pick up the appropriate colored card from their department and drop it into a "call" box in the department visited. These "call" boxes can then be emptied each night and the cards coded with the identifying number of the department in which each was found. At the end of the allotted time period the cards can be run through the computer for a printout of an accurate traffic pattern of people and document movement.

If the department head's requirements and the objective tests of departmental needs are the same, the layout should be planned accordingly unless new systems for paper handling and communications are to be installed which would have an effect on these proximity needs. If the test results are at odds with the department head's ideas this does not automatically mean that the test results should prevail. The department head may have quite logical reasons for the stated proximity needs, which should be followed in planning the layout despite the results of the test. At any rate, the test must be reviewed with department heads and with management for the impact the results may have on possible changes in systems and procedures as well as on layout.

The eventual translation of departmental relationships to building profile (floor-to-floor relationship) and to actual floor layout will be done in conjunction with the decision to be made later concerning renting or building. At that time, the problems of vertical versus horizontal traffic will be studied for the impact each will have on personnel, material, and communication requirements.

The answers to question 3 will help to determine the need for a separate department reception room as well as the amount and kind of seating that would be required in it, and the need for interview rooms, application processing rooms, vendor sample rooms, bid opening rooms, and other areas for public use. Special facilities of this sort would be used in personnel departments, purchasing departments, buying offices, advertising departments, etc.

Because much conference room space stays unused a great deal of the time, it becomes important to validate the need for such a facility. That includes the validation of conference areas in private offices as well as separate conference and meeting rooms. The answers to question 4 will help to make such a determination and, in the process, show what equipment is required for many of these meeting rooms, such as projection equipment, screens, chalkboards, corkboards, presentation rails, audio-visual equipment, and any other meeting aids that may be needed. Figure 4-5 shows a suggested form for charting existing and required facilities. Very often the information gathered results in several departments sharing a meeting room and working out an agreed-upon schedule for its use. At other times, a department may get its own conference room but end up sharing movable equipment with other departments. In any event, answers to question 4 will reveal the true need for conference space, where it could best be placed to serve the most people with the least possible waste of space, and how to provide the best kind of equipment to serve the needs of the users.

Figure 4-5   CONFERENCE/MEETING ROOM FACILITIES CHART

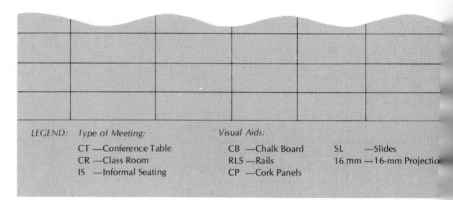

| | | | EXISTING | | |
Dept.	Purpose of meeting	Location	Size of room	Length of meeting	Frequency
Sales	Sales Reports	Conf.Rm.A	350	3 hrs	Monthly—1st Mon. A.M.
Research	New Data	Conf.Rm.B	250	2 hrs	Weekly Tues.10

These questions, particularly those dealing with the length of meetings, frequency, number of people attending the type of meetings, equipment and future requirements, should be carefully and accurately answered. The most important information to be gathered concerning the conference/meeting rooms is the use the rooms will get measured against the use they could get if they became shared facilities.

LEGEND: Type of Meeting: Visual Aids:

CT —Conference Table   CB —Chalk Board   SL   —Slides
CR —Class Room   RLS —Rails   16 mm —16-mm Projection
IS —Informal Seating   CP —Cork Panels

A "yes" answer to question 5 means there is both a heating and ventilating problem and a security problem to be solved. Most modern buildings, particularly those in which space would be rented, limit their air conditioning to five workdays a week starting at 7:30 or 8 A.M. and stopping at 6 P.M. Special provision must therefore be made for people who work at night and/or over weekends. Exactly how that can be done is discussed later. Because receptionists are usually not kept on for overtime work and the building staff is usually reduced to one employee during off hours, special security measures have to be taken for the safety of those people who work overtime shifts. This too will be discussed in Chapter 6 along with the solutions for any security problems that a "yes" answer to question 6 may raise.

Questions 7 through 10 deal mainly with operational problems and the answers could lead to further studies of possible changes in systems and procedures, all of which will be covered in Chapter 5.

No. of people attending	Type of meeting	Audio-vis. equipment		Audio-vis. equipment	Remarks
			REQUIRED		
			Locate		
10	CT	CB 16mm	DPT	Same + Mult. Sl.	Need room to seat 30 people—class rm.
5	IS	CP	NI	Same	

Armed with this information it will then be up to the planner and management to persuade departments to share these rooms with other departments. Sharing can be accomplished by fiat, but is much more effective when done willingly. A great advantage to sharing is that much more and better quality audio-visual equipment can be made available in rooms that are used constantly. Also equipment can then be built in as part of the room rather than suffer the abuse that is usually the lot of portable equipment.

DPT —In or Near Department
NI —Not Important

Questions 11 and 12 are general in nature and are designed to encourage department heads to verbalize about the future as they would like to see it.

Figure 4-6 shows the form to be used with question 13. On it the department head should list all departmental personnel by job title, the number of people presently in each work category, and the type of space each occupies. In the "Proposed Number" columns there should be listed the number of people anticipated in each category for each of the years shown. The first column, unheaded, is for coordination with the inventory. The pertinent number or numbers shown in the Inventory Sheet relating to this department's personnel should be entered here in order to coordinate the two forms. The proposed type of space and footage can be filled in later, after new space standards have been determined. The "Remarks" column is used by the interviewer whenever the validity of projections is questionable and subject to further management discussion.

Figure 4-6 DEPARTMENTAL PERSONNEL FORM

DEPARTMENT:			DEP'T. HEAD					DATE:			
PRESENT			**ANTICIPATED NUMBER OF PEOPLE**						**TABULATION FOR YEAR 19___**		
										Footages	
Job title	Type of space	No.of pers.	19___	19___	19___	19___	No.of pers.	Type of space	Remarks	Unit	Total

Type of Space: PO —Private Office
PO/2 —Pvt. Off. for 2
BSO/4 —Bankscreen Off. for 4

DEPARTMENT HEAD: Do not fill in beyond "ANTICIPATED NUMBER" columns. Planner will fill in first column with I.D. number from inventory form. Please account for any personnel listed as part of your department but working elsewhere.

ADDITIONAL FACILITIES

To take full advantage of this opportunity for change there should be a review of possible new facilities. Some of these might add to overall efficiency while others would provide personnel amenities that could be helpful in boosting morale. Whatever the reason for accepting or rejecting a facility, thought should be given to creating a list of ideas for management consideration. The following list, although certainly not complete, contains a number of things most companies do not have but that could be enjoyed under the proper circumstances:

- *Airstrip or helicopter pad.* This can be extremely useful for companies with their own planes or whose clients have planes of their own.

- *Auditorium.* A facility of this kind is valuable only if it can be utilized often enough each year to warrant spending the money necessary to build it, house it, and maintain it. Useful for large company meetings and stockholder meetings, an auditorium can be offered as a public relations gesture to the community for its use, for charitable purposes, and for demonstrations of company products.

- *Exhibit facilities.* These too can be for company use and/or community use.

- *Barber shop.* Wherever one has been installed it has been greatly appreciated by personnel. In some instances its use has been confined to executives.

- *Gasoline station/service station.* This can be a service that does no more than sell gasoline to employees or it can be a full service repair facility. Whatever the extent of the service offered it has proved to be a welcome time-saving device for employees and, in some cases, a definite cost-saving "dividend."

- *Golf practice range/golf course.* Luxury items that can have great public relations impact.

- *Health center.* Rest rooms, sick bay, nurses in attendance, and a doctor on call are not unusual. What would be unusual is the introduction of facilities such as a gymnasium (for handball, squash, volley ball), a sauna, and a swimming pool.

- *Public information center.* This depends largely on the geographical location of the facilities and/or the business of the company. Centers like this have served as travel information centers and locality information centers including information about points of interest, food, lodging, etc. They have also served as centers for conducting building and plant guided tours.

- *Shops.* These too depend upon the building location. If it is in the suburbs and inaccessible to a public shopping center, shops in the building can provide those things most needed by working people: cleaning, laundry, shoe repair, card shops, specialty shops, food stores, magazines, books, etc. These can be made available to the general public as well as company personnel.

5 Planning Operational Changes

The operation of any company can be made more efficient by improving the way in which it handles paper, filing, reproduction, mail, and all the other functions that are part of its normal business day. Many companies try to keep up-to-date on the progress made in office systems and procedures. Any attempt to make changes on a hit-or-miss basis can be costly and disruptive. A move to new quarters or a plan to change the physical layout of existing offices provides a wonderful opportunity to update operating systems and procedures and thus get rid of many of the bad habits that a company can acquire over the years.

The study of existing systems should not be confined just to improving the old methods of doing things. It should help to determine which things that have not been done might be made part of the company operations. The areas where changes could be made fall into a few broad categories, which are labeled only for convenience of study. With rare exceptions, meaningful changes in any of the listed items will have a "triple-barreled" effect on company efficiency because each should provide better utilization of floor space, people, and equipment. For example, the introduction of a system of word processing will have a considerable effect on the number of secretaries, clerks, and typists required, and it will reduce the amount of space needed to house these people. Although it will eliminate the cost of furniture that would otherwise have been purchased, new, more efficient equipment will have to be introduced. The savings in rent and payroll will be an extra dividend because the new equipment will reduce the cost of producing a superior piece of manageable paper.

It is important, therefore, that the study of possible operational changes take place concurrently with the study of departments, service areas, and personnel needs. Only in this way can the conclusions be coordinated with all the other planning aspects of the project and be made part of the preliminary space-planning concepts.

The following list includes the operational areas that should be considered for change:

1. *Paper management*
   a. Word processing
   b. Records management
      - File location
      - Paper handling
      - Mail room
      - Satellite service centers
      - Records retention
      - Microfilming
      - Filing systems and equipment
      - Forms
      - Duplication
   c. Operations manual
2. *Supplies*
3. *Data processing*
4. *Communications*
   a. Telephone
   b. Intercommunications
   c. Graphics communications (FAX)
   d. Audio-visual communications
5. *Company services*
   a. Library
   b. Conference/meeting rooms
   c. Showrooms/salesrooms
6. *Security*

Because all planning efforts are so interrelated, it is important that careful notation be made of the need for any odd or unusual physical facilities to accommodate operational changes. A new paper-handling system may require the piercing of floor slabs for a dumbwaiter or paper-carrying conveyors. A new filing system may require additional floor-load capacities. A new duplicating system may require large photo equipment that can be accommodated only with special ceiling heights. Any or all of these requirements would have to be made known to the space planner and architect, first for budgeting and then for eventual inclusion in the construction plans.

For the same reason the study of all the items listed must include an analysis of any electrical, air conditioning, and ventilating requirements in excess of normal building standards. The need for any such excesses would also have to be made known so that they too could be included on final construction plans once their budgeted costs had been approved. Special furniture, furnishings, and/or equipment that might be needed would automatically be noted for study, but here again, care must be taken that information concerning such needs is properly disseminated. Items to be purchased would have to be part of the purchasing program. Items to be designed and/or constructed and installed would have to be included on the working drawings and design details.

In each of the areas to be studied there will be some kind of equipment to be considered and compared to similar equipment. This will be true whether it be storage shelving, typewriters, or highly technical electronic computers. Salespeople can be extremely helpful in supplying information about the particular products they are selling, but where possible an objective viewpoint should be sought before a purchase is made. An outside consultant who is being used for a specific task study should be able to supply the objective view. When a study is being done in-house, it is a good idea to check references among the users of the equipment being considered.

When making plans for systems and procedures changes, a judgment must be made of the capacity for company personnel to work comfortably with the new system. Failure to make this evaluation or to train and motivate the staff properly could seriously hamper the successful operation of many of the planned innovations. New methods and procedures, especially those that require a learning process and changes in job responsibilities, will always evoke negative responses from personnel at all work levels. This very normal resistance must be anticipated and rendered as harmless as possible through a positive introduction of the new system to be adopted. The staff must be told that management, after lengthy study, has determined that the new system is good, and they must be told why it is good. Furthermore, it must be made clear that the system is not being tested, but is being installed.

PAPER MANAGEMENT

The first, most obvious area for effective change is in the study of *paper management*. It is the lifeblood of any business operation and, as such, is very much in need of a permanent anticoagulant. Control over the flow of paper must start at the source, the originator and the secretary, and continue on through the production process: filing, retrieval, duplication, handling, form design, storage, and eventually, disposal.

Word Processing

In the beginning is the secretary! Learning what the secretarial job is, how it is done, why it is done, and how it may be more effectively accomplished is the primary goal of the *word-processing* study.

Such a study, by the way, should not be confined to large companies. There seems to be an idea that only companies occupying more than 50,000 sq ft should bother with such a study. It is true that operational changes will have more dramatic results if the subject company is a large one. Cutting fifty secretaries from a secretarial payroll of two hundred with no loss in production has to look startling on a balance sheet, but that does not mean that procedural changes cannot be equally important to a small company as well.

The word-processing study, like the departmental interviews and the inventories, must be conducted only after the departments to be studied and the people to be interviewed within each department have been notified of the study, the manner in which it will be conducted, and the help that is expected from personnel in order to make the study an effective one. This advance notification should take place whether the study will be completely staff-conducted or managed by an outside consultant. If an outside consultant firm is to be used, the project director must assign an in-house coordinator to assist. The coordinator should be thoroughly conversant with the existing systems and procedures. The first job of such a person would be to explain the existing organization and supply whatever background information is available that may have a bearing on the study to be undertaken. The second would be to arrange for and schedule all interviews to help validate the information gathered.

Mention was made earlier of the effect that systems changes have on the amount of space to be utilized. These changes will also have a tremendous bearing on the determination of the "planning concept" that will eventually be established for the company. Although discussion of these concepts, such as open planning and office landscape, will take place in Chapter 7, it is just as well to mention here the impact the systems studies can have in determining not only the amount of space that will be required but the manner in which that space can be planned.

Information for a word-processing study should be gathered from those who originate paperwork (the writers of correspondence, reports, memos, proposals, etc.) and those who produce it (secretaries and typists). Figure 5-1 shows a form with the typical kinds of questions that should be asked of all those who originate paperwork. These questions and those asked of the "producers" (Figure 5-2) are obviously aimed at determining the amount and kind of paperwork the secretary produces, where it goes, and what else the secretary does or can do or should do. If, after an analysis of the work flow and personnel activity, the interviews indicate that secretarial duties will be performed more efficiently by reassignments, retraining, and some job elimination, the word-processing study should then dig further into the whole process of originating and producing paper. Dictating, typing, and all the other tasks performed by originators and secretaries should be accurately logged on a minute-to-minute basis with the time broken down into such task components as dictating, lines typed, correction, editing, proofreading, and retyping.

Upon completion of the study, recommendations can be made for task reassignments

Figure 5-1 WORD PROCESSING STUDY

71

Planning Operational Changes

Originator Questionnaire

DEPARTMENT_____ DATE_____

NAME_____ INTERVIEWED BY_____

  Job function_____

  Name of Secretary_____

  Shared? yes/no   If yes, with whom?_____

Type of material originated:

1. Correspondence	_____%	5. Manuals	_____%
2. Proposals	_____%	6. Specifications	_____%
3. Memos	_____%	7. _____	_____%
4. Reports	_____%	8. _____	_____%

How is your time spent	Day	Week	Month
1. Originating material	_____%	_____%	_____%
2. Phoning	_____%	_____%	_____%
3. Research	_____%	_____%	_____%
4. Meeting	_____%	_____%	_____%
5. _____	_____%	_____%	_____%
6. _____	_____%	_____%	_____%

How is your work originated

  1. Machine-dictated _____%

  2. Secretary-dictated _____%

  3. Long-hand _____%

  4. _____ _____%

How much is originated outside of the office _____%

Does your secretary originate any material—yes/no

  If yes, what and how much _____

What functions that you carry out could your secretary handle for you _____

and eliminations and for the procurement of new equipment, based on a comparative analysis of the efficiencies and the costs of the existing versus the proposed procedures. Such a report should include the methodology for accomplishing this changeover as far as staff education and equipment installation are concerned. It should also include recommendations for the number of word-processing centers that should be set up and indicate the amount of space required for each. The manner in which a word-processing system is introduced is of vital importance to its initial well-being and its continued health. It is not a static system and should not be treated as such. The ability of both management and staff to grow with the constant changes that will take place in the "art" of word processing will depend upon the manner in which the system is first implemented.

Figure 5-2   WORD PROCESSING STUDY

Secretarial Questionnaire

DEPARTMENT_____ DATE_____

NAME_____ INTERVIEWED BY_____

Secretary to_____ Equipment_____

Assign a frequency percentage of your time by day, week, and month to those of the following functions which you perform. Please put a zero next to those that are not your responsibility:

	Day	Week	Month
1. Take dictation	_____%	_____%	_____%
2. Type: Correspondence	_____%	_____%	_____%
Proposals	_____%	_____%	_____%
Memos	_____%	_____%	_____%
Reports	_____%	_____%	_____%
Other	_____%	_____%	_____%
3. Proofread	_____%	_____%	_____%
4. Mail: Open	_____%	_____%	_____%
Sort	_____%	_____%	_____%
Deliver	_____%	_____%	_____%
5. Photocopy	_____%	_____%	_____%
6. Meetings: Arrange	_____%	_____%	_____%
Attend	_____%	_____%	_____%
7. Telephone: Outgoing	_____%	_____%	_____%
Incoming	_____%	_____%	_____%
8. Travel: Arrange itinerary	_____%	_____%	_____%
Make reservations	_____%	_____%	_____%
9. Filing	_____%	_____%	_____%
10. Personal services	_____%	_____%	_____%
11. _____	_____%	_____%	_____%

What do you like to do?
What do you do best?

Does anyone help you with your work? yes/no
    If yes, who and how often?

Please comment on—work you think you should not be doing.
              —work you think you should be doing.
              —any other aspects of your work.

As mentioned earlier, despite all the reports indicating obvious advantages of the new system, there are always cries of anguish when all levels of company personnel realize some of the basic implications of the changeover. The elimination of jobs and the sudden need for seemingly entrenched people to have to retrain and learn new skills are bad enough. But the awful realization that "status" seems to be endangered with the disappearance of many cherished "private" secretaries can be a traumatic experience unless management has done the necessary job of preparing its people for the future that is upon them.

As for the advantages, there are no meaningful "rules of thumb" for "guesstimating" the savings to be made by the introduction of word processing. Consultants lay claim to a possible annual saving of 30 to 40 percent on paperwork production. A rather typical example, which seems to bear out this contention, is the recently studied company that had 300 originators and 200 secretaries. The study report done for them indicated the possible elimination of ninety secretaries. By allotting $10,000 per secretary per year and amortizing the $275,000 cost for required new equipment over a 5-year period, the annual savings would be $845,000. This, of course, is a very basic calculation, which does not account for any saving in such things as rent and fringe benefits. Whether savings of this magnitude are achieved or not is not the compelling reason for installing a word-processing system. The savings would be but an "extra added attraction" on top of the huge gains to be made from the more efficient utilization of personnel, space, and equipment.

Records Management

The next area of study within the overall category of paper management is *records management*. There is, naturally, a definite relationship between records management and the word-processing procedure. The paper produced under word processing is by its nature a record to be managed and to be integrated and coordinated into a records management system that includes filing, retention policies, paper handling, forms design, and duplicating.

Much of the work done analyzing existing systems and procedures for records handling can be done with and through most of the people who are involved in the word-processing study. Eventually, when the new systems and procedures are in operation, they will require day-to-day management. How much time this will take— and how many people will be involved in this systems management role—should be determined as early as possible. It would then be advisable to get these people involved at the very beginning of the systems studies. In any event, the records management coordinator, working with or without an outside consultant group, must arrange for the announcement to company personnel that a records survey is to be made. They should be told why it is being made, how it will be made, and the kind of cooperation that will be required from each person questioned. The heads of the departments that will be involved in the survey will appoint appropriate people from their departments to assist, and the total survey program will be described to all these people. Once again a questionnaire form should be given to the responsible personnel for processing prior to the coordinator/consultant visit to each department. Figure 5-3 shows a typical preliminary records survey form.

The information asked for in a records survey should include the type of records being kept (correspondence, personnel files, purchase orders, etc.) and the time period covered. It should also be specific about the kind of filing equipment being used and the

Figure 5-3 PRELIMINARY RECORDS SURVEY

Department:										Date:	
Information from:							Interviewed by:				
Location of records:											
Type of records	Dates		Volume	Size	Equip.				Use			Retention	
	From	To			V	L	S	M	O	I	D	Period	Reason

CODE: *Volume*—Lineal footage or number of drawers   *Equipment*—V, Vertical; L, Lateral; S, Shelf;
       Size—Legal or letter   M, Microfilm.
                                                                 Use—O, Often; I, Infrequent; D, Dead file.

number of file drawers (or lineal feet of shelving) being used to house the records. Next,

in order to judge possible location of the files, it is important to know whether the records should be in the department—if so, why, and if not, how frequently the files may be used. In connection with this, note must be made of those records so vital to the company that they must be permanently retained—and where. Then there must be knowledge of the existing records-retention policy, if there is one. The question is aimed at finding out the number of years that records should be kept and whether this is company policy or policy mandated by government regulations. When all this information is analyzed, consideration must then be given to the following:

File Location.   This must be coordinated with word processing, with required file use, and with a records retention program. From the analysis of all three of them will come the decision as to how to house files and where to house them: in a central filing area, in file rooms on each floor requiring them, in the basement, or in off-the-premises dead storage areas. The final decision could be for one of these solutions or for some combination of part or all of them.

Paper Handling.   Basic to any effective systems and procedures changes that may be made in paper management must be a thorough understanding of the route paper takes as it travels through an organization. What happens to incoming mail, how does it get where it is first supposed to go, and how many other people work on it or must see it before it gets answered and/or filed? How does paper that originates within the organization get where it is supposed to go, how many people see or act on it before it gets there, and how many work on it before it gets mailed out and/or filed?

The results of charting the course of each kind of "paper" not only will aid greatly in deciding file locations but will also be the major factor in determining what the mail room will be like, where it will be, and what method will be used to deliver and distribute paper. Paper delivery, for example, can be done by messengers, by conveyor belts, through a pneumatic tube system, or by one of a number of automated, trackriding carriers capable of vertical and horizontal movement.

Mail Room.   How the mail room will be planned and what kind of equipment will be used in it will depend on whether all mail, incoming and outgoing, will be processed completely or partially in one room. That decision will be made when the quantity of mail to be handled is known and questions such as the following have been answered:

- Will the mail be opened, stamped in, logged, and then delivered to the individual or department to whom it is addressed?
- Or will it be sent to the individual departments for that kind of processing?
- Will internal mail, memos, etc., be handled by the mail room?

• Will outgoing mail be machine-stamped in the mail room with postal charges levied against the originating department?

Satellite Service Centers.   Not necessarily confined to paper management, these centers offer another example of the need for coordinating effort in planning office space. In examining the whole subject of operational changes, thought should be given to the strategic placement of these centers on each floor, on every other floor, or wherever their placement(s) would be most effective. The operational elements that could be included in such service centers are

- Area filing
- Mail room services
- Supplies
- Office copying
- Automated typing

and any other of the central services that might be more efficiently handled in strategically placed locations, rather than one, possibly remote, area.

Records Retention.   With or without government regulations that mandate the period of records retention, a company policy should be established and rigidly policed. The number of years that records should be kept is ultimately a decision that management will make with or without legal or accounting help. Experience seems to indicate that very few records have any value after 6 years and almost none have value after 10 years. The exception would be those papers that fall under the heading of "vital documents." What portion of these can go into dead storage and which documents have to be kept readily available will dictate location. The overall policy concerning the length of time for paper retention will have a definite bearing on the efficacy of a microfilming program.

Microfilming.   Microfilming could be instituted for security reasons (storage of copies of documents in an area other than the one in which the originals are stored) or to replace and reduce the amount of space needed to retain paper that must be kept for some length of time. It could then provide, also, a method for rapid retrieval of stored material. Whether microfilming would be economically sound or not would depend upon a very simple arithmetic computation: the rent being paid per square foot for each four-drawer file cabinet (microfilm storage is approximately 2 to 3 percent of that cost) modified by the cost of microfilming the contents of that four-drawer cabinet (approximately $200) plus the cost of required retrieval equipment purchased or rented as compared to the cost of manual retrieval.

   In considering the financial advantages (or disadvantages) of microfilming, all the latest available equipment should be understood and explored. In a comparatively few years vast improvements have taken place in the microfilm process. Changes in cameras and film processing, plus the introduction of COM (Computer Output Microfilm) recording equipment and rapid retrieval units, have added sophistication and versatility to the microfilm system. COM occupies a very small percentage of the space required for regular paper printouts. Used properly, it can help reduce the costs associated with printing and distribution, manual sorting and filing, and required storage.

Filing Systems and Equipment.   The development of a new filing system and the choice of the equipment that would best serve that system become possible after the acceptance of word processing, the establishment of a records retention policy, the establishment of file locations, and agreement on the desirability for and the extent of a microfilm program.

The ''hardware'' for implementing a filing system will include the filing units, folders, envelopes, tabs, and all other paper ''containers'' that might sit within those units. The software will include the systems for coding, titling, and indexing all filed material for easy identification and all other descriptive material that will be part of a records operations manual.

Filing equipment comes in all shapes and forms as well as varying degrees of electric and electronic sophistication. Starting with the old, familiar, four-drawer file, equipment has developed to the point where it is not an exaggeration to say that a push of the button brings any needed file folder to the desk. Whether it be shelf files, cabinet files, banks of mobile files, rotary files, or automated files, the kind or kinds to be used should be those that best meet specific records management requirements.

Forms.   Part of any records management program must be a study of all the forms in use, the reasons for their existence, and how they came into being. The purpose of such a study would be to help combine as many forms as possible, simplify and revise existing forms that will continue to be used, and create forms where new ones are indicated. In the process the standardization of graphics and standardization of form verbiage should help greatly in a continuing form program. The kind and size of paper and the methods for reproduction must be determined along with the decisions concerning in-house versus outside form printing.

Duplication.   Duplication is a service arm of the whole paper management process. If a company's duplication problems require it, a study could include printing, office copying, and reproduction of engineering and architectural drawings. (Long-distance duplication through the use of facsimile telecommunication equipment will be part of the whole communications subject.) Printing equipment runs from simple spirit duplicating and stencil printing through very sophisticated offset machines, some of which are linked to their own electrostatic platemakers. In addition there is a wide variety of equipment for photocomposition which many in-house printing "shops" use to make their service more complete.

A complete analysis and charting of office copying, printing, and reproduction requirements would have to be made to help determine the equipment best suited to meet these needs. The study of duplication would also have to include a comparative analysis of collating and binding methods and equipment. Recommendations would have to take into consideration the advisability of placing some office copying equipment in the proposed satellite service centers. The ideal layout for each center and/or for a duplicating "shop" would also be included in the specific recommendations to be made to management.

Operations Manual

The *operations manual* should describe all equipment, systems and procedures of the records management program and explain all aspects of indexing, coding, retention, purging, cross-reference filing, logging, routing, etc. It should set up complete guidelines for implementing the systems, the controls necessary to keep them running smoothly, and the personnel responsibilities for each step of the processes, including the constant maintenance of the program on a current basis. It should, in short, be the "Bible" of not only the records management program but the whole paper management system as well.

Cost Analysis

The final step of the paper management study must be a complete *cost analysis* of each aspect of the proposed program: file location, paper handling, record retention, microfilming, filing systems, and all other parts of the program. In each case the elements subject to cost analysis are the same: a comparison of existing versus recommended systems based on the cost of software, hardware, and personnel training, the cost of space to house the operations, and the cost of people needed to run them, including any professional consultant fees that might have more than a "one-shot" impact.

Since this comparative analysis will usually include the savings to be gained through the elimination of line personnel, it is important to remember that no systems change will remain effectively operable unless someone in management is made responsible for controlling it. Whether one person has control or whether each specific part of the program is under the control of a different person, the cost of these task controllers must be a part of the analysis.

A cost analysis of this kind should be made in connection with all contemplated operational changes.

SUPPLIES

The next area to be studied for possible changes and improvements in operation should be the manner in which *supplies* are handled. Relatively few companies require separate facilities for supplies alone. Most combine them with a mail room and/or a central printing area. When company offices occupy a great deal of space, supplies can be distributed more readily through the satellite service areas. Each such center would carry a forward stock of supplies sufficient to take care of supply needs within its area for a predetermined length of time. Stock could then be replenished on a regular schedule. The service center personnel would be responsible for controlling the inventory of supplies, office copying, mail, and/or any other services designated.

The kinds of things that make up a company's supplies, how they are chosen, how prices are negotiated, and how they are purchased are not subjects appropriate for this book. It is urged, however, that much thought be given to the standardization of items and to a program that will be specific in determining the desirable amount of inventory of each item that should be stocked. Care should be taken to see that all required supplies are on hand as they are needed. Such a program will make it possible to determine the proper amount of space required for both central and satellite storage areas.

DATA PROCESSING

Another major area for study in which operational efficiencies can be effected is *data processing*. This may be the study of an existing system that could lead to the use of more sophisticated equipment, or it might be the introduction of automation and a data processing system that is entirely new to the company. Like all other systems and procedures studies, this will deal with the present work load, how many people work at it, how long it takes to do, what equipment is being used to accomplish it, what space is required for this effort, and what else could be done that is not being done. The existing "condition" must then be analyzed against the anticipated efficiencies of new equipment and its cost, the personnel required to operate it, the space needed to house it, and the additional, helpful information that may be supplied by new equipment.

Once the overall program has been determined, decisions must be made concerning the space required, the location of these areas, the kinds of floor, walls, and ceilings needed, and whatever unusual air conditioning and electrical specifications may be required for the space. The elements that could occupy the space include a computer equipment room, offices for programmers, a tape vault, and a supply room for equipment parts, data processing paper, and forms storage. Planning should also take into consideration the need for future expansion (or contraction) of the area. Location would depend upon the need for proximity to other departments, the desire to display this facility to the outside public, or the possibility that this could be housed in something less than prime space, particularly when the company is renting office space in a central area of a major city.

Flooring, if the electrical load for equipment is heavy, should be raised, with the floor panels specified in easy-to-handle sizes allowing for rapid repairs, additions, and/or shifting of equipment as needed. The ceilings should be easy to clean and of a material that will not produce excessive dust. It, too, should be flexible enough to allow for rapid changes in lighting fixture locations or for fixture additions. The partitions should provide for maximum sound control and serve as a thermal barrier. If the area is to be displayed to the outside public, glass panels for viewing will have to be an integral part of the partitions.

Air conditioning and humidification should be engineered for both creature comfort and equipment performance. Electricity should be planned to carry the load requirements of the equipment, air conditioning and heating, humidifiers, and lighting.

Fire controls, security, and the fact that data processing may be a two- or three-shift operation are all things that must be considered in the overall planning of such a facility. These possibilities could have a direct bearing on location considerations.

COMMUNICATIONS

Another operational element of major importance is *communications.* It represents an office function that must be studied as part of any office move. The more thorough the study, the greater the potential yield of savings and efficiency. Under this broad heading are included telephone, intercom, facsimile transmission by wire or radio, and audio-visual systems as a tool of communication with company personnel or clients.

The need for up-to-the-minute, in-depth study is rather obvious because of the almost minute-by-minute changes that take place in equipment development. Starting with mouth-to-ear communication right through to telegraph, telephone, radio, television, satellites, laser, optical fibers, and whatever it is that is now being worked on behind those closed laboratory doors, the future of communications becomes its past very rapidly.

Telephone

The *telephone* survey, similar to the survey made for word processing and records management, must start with the originating source—the telephone user. Whether the telephone expert is in-house or a retained consultant, the purpose of his or her study should be known in advance by those who will be asked to participate. Starting with the telephone operator and then covering all the chief telephone users, the company requirements for telephones, tie lines, conference calls, call transfers, hold mechanisms, call pick-ups, forwarding, WATS lines, etc., must be carefully charted against the efficiencies of the present system. The new system can then be engineered, specifications prepared for the desired equipment, and formal bids requested of the Bell System and whatever other interconnect systems can meet the requirements and specifications. Submitted bids should then be analyzed for both installation and in-use cost comparisons. Bell equipment is, of course, rented from the Bell Telephone Company, while private vendors' equipment is either purchased or bought on a lease or a lease-to-purchase program.

Part of the planning for any telephone system should include a decision about public telephones. Consideration should be given to such questions as whether there should be pay phones for the outside public, for employee use, including any disabled employees, and for delivery people.

Approval of a system and a supplier means that immediate coordination between supplier, planner, and telephone consultant must be established so that all construction aspects of the new system can be made part of the working drawings.

A telephone system such as Centrex or one of the many interconnect systems might be completely new to the company, and a call coming directly to each phone from the outside, without having to go through a switchboard or equipment such as call directors, might be strange to company personnel. The consultant should conduct training sessions for those who will be using the equipment and for those whose calls may be affected by it. When the company moves into its new home, everyone should know all that he or she must know to operate the new telephonic communication "machine."

There is a telecommunications service offered by a group known as BIC (Building Industry Consulting Service), funded by the American Telephone and Telegraph Company and offered at no charge to planners and architects. Consulted prior to the completion of plans for a building, they will help determine the size of required equipment, rooms, or closets and the most efficient plans for conduits and ducts to accommodate the initial and eventual overall telephone system. Called in early enough they can help see to it that most of the built-in capacities become part of the basic building and that later changes can be accomplished at minor costs.

Intercommunications

Intercommunications in most large installations becomes a function of the telephone system alone or the telephone system in conjunction with the audio-visual installations. There are intercom systems that are completely separate from the telephone, with equipment of their own in the form of "squawk boxes," phones, or a combination of the two. These can be used to fill specific needs such as rapid and very frequent communication to a service area, communication between key people for specific reasons, and security phones for direct, immediate communication between selected people and areas.

Graphics Communications

Graphics communications (FAX) is still another part of the communications problem that requires analytical study. It, too, is a field undergoing rapid changes that have added greatly to its sophistication and efficiency. The research and development in this field is aimed at reducing equipment cost, transmitting cost, speed of transmission, and clarity of reproduction. The methods for transmitting include a variety of facsimile equipment using the telephone as the transmitting instrument, the Telex or teletypewriter available through Western Union, satellite network transmission, and electronic mail service which, at this writing, is far enough advanced developmentally to be feasible for use by the time this is read. In addition, there is another exciting development which will add to the general usefulness of facsimile transmission: the ability to transmit messages to a computer memory system along with instructions to transmit at a specific time or times.

Audio-Visual Communications

Audio-visual communications, used in the business world, is basically an instrument for instruction. It may present the information from which management will make its decisions, "show and tell" how the company is doing, instruct salespeople, train personnel for a multiplicity of tasks, as well as sell the company "products" to its customers.

What has to be said, to whom it must be said, and where it should be said are all basic determinations that aid in deciding which audio-visual equipment should be used, how space should be planned for it, and how costs should be estimated. The audio-visual presentation can be via closed circuit television, beamed directly (or taped for later beaming) to branches all over the world, or it can be a hand-held pointer aimed at a chart pinned to a cork or chalk board. An experienced audio-visual communications expert should be consulted to help a company find better ways of doing what has to be done and, at the same time, expose it to the many things it might be doing. How far the company goes in an audio-visual program will depend entirely on an analysis of the gains to be made and the costs involved in making them. A responsible consultant knows that whatever glamor there is in an audio-visual "showplace" must come completely from its ability to fill a need.

Any audio-visual communications study must also be tied very closely to the study of conference/meeting rooms, described below and in Chapter 4.

Everything having to do with an audio-visual installation, whether it is only a railing on which to place presentation boards or a sophisticated slide, movie, and television combination, will have an impact on space planning and design. Information concerning it must be circulated as soon as decisions are made. Those decisions can affect architectural effort, structural and mechanical engineering, space planning, design, finishing materials, cabinet work, furniture, and of course, equipment.

The last category for systems and procedures study comes under the umbrella heading of "services" and includes such things as libraries, conference/meeting rooms, salesrooms, and showrooms.

Library

The effectiveness of an existing company *library* is fairly easy to measure by studying a list (which can be supplied by the company librarian) of the people who use it, how often each uses it, what books or periodicals are used, where they are used (in the library, in the user's office, or at home), and for how long. Users (and nonusers who might visit the facility) can be questioned concerning any other libraries they may be using or about any books or periodicals they may like to be able to use but which are not available to them through the company library. At the same time, information can be gathered concerning the availability of required books and periodicals from nearby public, private, or university libraries. If the information required is readily obtainable from outside sources within a reasonable time span, it may be possible to decrease the size of the existing library or eliminate it entirely. Should it be advisable to expand the facility after studying its potential use, it would be good to retain a library consultant (unless the company librarian is sufficiently knowledgeable) to help set up a total information system and train personnel to maintain it.

Conference/Meeting Rooms

The potential savings in space use alone through a proper evaluation of the use of *conference/meeting rooms* can be rather tremendous. This was covered in Chapter 4, but it may be helpful at this point (particularly if there is great need for conference/meeting rooms) to chart a program for their use. Figure 4-5, a conference/meeting room facilities chart, is a suggested form for this purpose. On it can be listed any special items to be designed and/or purchased for meeting rooms and any audio-visual equipment that may be required. This should be coordinated with the audio-visual study and can be a checklist for the acquisition of conference room furniture and equipment and can eventually be used when room use schedules are determined.

Showrooms/Salesrooms

A strict interpretation of the company services classification would require the inclusion of *showrooms,* where company merchandise is displayed and sold to buyers for wholesale and retail outlets and *salesrooms,* where manufacturers' salespeople come to show their wares to company buyers. The latter is a facility usually connected with a "buying office," i.e., a company that does the buying for a group or chain of stores. Both the showroom(s) and the salesroom(s) are quite specialized, and each situation that requires the use of one or the other type of room must be studied for its own particular needs. One element common to all such facilities and appropriate to the subject matter of this book is the percentage of use each room would get during a business day. Historically, such rooms are used for a limited number of hours each day or week and usually on a predictable or preset schedule. Where possible these rooms should be set up as dual-purpose rooms in order to get the maximum use for the rent dollar spent. Showrooms can very often double as private offices for sales managers or salespeople. Through the use of a movable wall system, salesrooms, used as such in the morning, can become classrooms, training rooms, or meeting rooms in the afternoon.

There are other service areas to be considered, areas in which effective changes can be made, but because each has, or could have, great impact on company personnel, they are more properly discussed in Chapter 6.

SECURITY

Before going on, one unpleasant subject must be raised—*security*. Security is really a two- or three-pronged problem. In addition to the corporate problem, there is also the personnel security problem and (where pertinent) the problem of building security. The latter two will be discussed in Chapter 6 and in "Project Staffing" at the end of Section V. Here it should be considered as yet another possible change in systems and procedures.

So much time has been devoted to the ways in which savings can be effected that it would be wrong to ignore the necessity of studying ways in which loss can be prevented. Losses can come about because of industrial sabotage, kickbacks, embezzlement, hijacking, employees' use of company time and materials for their own benefit, outright stealing of supplies and products, and a host of other unfortunate practices.

To institute preventative measures can be simple in some cases, involving little more than alarm systems, new key systems, electronic controls, or better guard control at entrances and exits. In other cases it can be far more involved, calling for carefully monitored controls of the flow of documents and merchandise. Judgment will have to be made as to the extent of the problems and the kind of help that will be required to solve them. If outside help is to be utilized, the consultant must be made completely familiar with the company operation and the procedures planned for those departments in which security problems are prevalent.

6 Planning for Personnel

Up to this point the emphasis of the planning study has almost exclusively been on effecting economies and increasing efficiencies through changes in location, equipment, filing systems, paper handling, word processing, and a host of other things that seem to have little to do with people. Actually, the whole subject of office planning must focus directly on the men and women who make it all happen. None of the systems and procedures that have been studied and planned and analyzed can possibly be implemented without people. Paper will not move, words will not get processed, orders will never get placed, and in fact, an office will never come into existence without people. No matter what your point of departure, no matter what your point of view, whether you believe that the organization revolves around the president or the office messenger, every person, in every job category, is a contributing factor helping to make the office entity run smoothly. To ignore anyone, president or office messenger, in the planning process can only weaken the impact of all that is done.

The chairman of the board of one of the top ten corporations of the world described it quite succinctly. Questioned about his ideas concerning the "image" that the new company offices should present to the public, he said:

This is a people business—our people. Whatever we do to create an environment, the chief beneficiaries must be our people, the people who make this business run. Anything we do to make their working hours more pleasant will quickly be recognized by the public, our customers, as being our "image."

To plan for people means to give consideration to the environment within which people will work, to the way in which the basic concepts of space are determined, to the sociological factors that will inhibit or enhance personnel, and to the company operational facilities that can add to or detract from the dignity of the employee.

OPERATIONAL CONSIDERATIONS

Since the last chapter dealt with planning operational changes as they affect departmental functions and company services, logic dictates that the first part of a study which involves planning for personnel should encompass those service areas that are set up, or could be set up, as an aid to company people.

Some of these service areas were suggested for consideration at the end of Chapter 4 when new facilities were discussed. They included interview rooms, a medical department, eating facilities, recreation, and travel aid. None of these is likely to produce the measurable savings possible with the operational improvement in other systems and procedures. Each could, however, have a very definite impact on staff relations and company morale.

Interview rooms and testing rooms, as part of the personnel department, usually present the first view that a job applicant gets of the company. Companies anxious to attract and keep the best talent available should put the department's reception, interview, and test areas to good use as a selling tool. They should not only reflect the attitude of the company to its employees, but also set the tone that reflects the quality and the efficiency of the company operation. The reception room should be large enough and there should be a sufficient number of seats available to make each applicant comfortable. The interview rooms should be so designed as to put the applicants at ease, while the testing rooms should put no other obstacles, except the test itself, before the test taker. Also, application forms and test forms should be designed for easy use and written for clear understanding. Phones, pay or otherwise, should be available for use by any applicant.

A *medical department* is completely discretionary. It need be no more than a rest room, sized and equipped to conform to local labor laws, or it can be a simple first aid station, staffed or unstaffed. Some companies provide a rest room or rooms with a nurse in constant attendance, while others have rest rooms, examination rooms, a nurse's office, and a doctor's office, with both nurse and doctor in constant attendance. Still others have a doctor available for a few hours each morning or afternoon or available only on call. To make a determination about this facility, past records of sickness and accidents should be studied and the desirability of giving yearly physical examinations to executives either on the premises or through outside medical help should be weighed. Medical advice could be sought when making these determinations. If there is any difficulty in contacting a doctor with group experience, the insurance company that handles the company's health and accident insurance should certainly be able to make one of their medical people available for consultation. Physical requirements for an in-house facility, such as water, gas, electricity, and x-ray equipment must become part of the final plan of the space, and information concerning them should be coordinated with the planner/architect.

Eating facilities can also be provided in all "sizes and shapes" ranging from a coffee pot in the supply room to a sit-down dining room. The list of possibilities could include one or more of the following:

1. Brown bag room(s) for those who bring lunch. This could also include coffee vending machines and refrigerators for cream, milk, sodas, etc.

2. Vending machines for soups, sandwiches, candies, cakes, and coffee.

3. A cafeteria that could be merely a cold sandwich, coffee, and soda installation or a full-service facility with hot foods, salads, desserts, and beverages.

4. Executive dining room(s) for executive staff use only, customer entertainment only, or a combination of the two. This could be one large room or a group of private rooms.

The possible combinations and permutations are limitless, and the choice should depend upon company policy. Because policy can be influenced by the availability of outside eating facilities, a study of this whole subject must include just such an analysis. Note must be made of the nieghborhood eating facilities, including available private clubs. Staff eating habits must be considered along with the desirability of staff and/or client luncheon meetings. The cost analysis should cover the various ways in which the facility might be run—by the company or by a food service concessionaire, as a profit-making venture or as a partially subsidized facility written off as a fringe benefit for employees. No cost analysis would be complete without calculating the rent for the space involved and any way in which rent could be shared if the space were given other uses in addition to dining.

When a cafeteria is so sized as to require two or three shifts, a particularly good way to get personnel out rapidly is to set up a *recreation* area next to the dining room. Such an area could contain Ping-Pong tables, pool tables, card tables, and lounge chairs. If the building is in a suburban area, outdoor recreation can be provided with shuffle-board, putting greens, Ping-Pong, and lounge chairs. If more vigorous exercise is desirable, bowling alleys, volleyball courts, tennis courts, paddle tennis courts, basket-ball courts, a driving range, or even a gymnasium can be provided.

If company personnel does a great amount of business travel, a study should be made of the way in which travel schedules, reservations, and ticketing would be most expeditiously handled. Should the company have its own *travel agency* or use an independent agency? Should it make this facility available to its personnel for other than business travel and, if so, should it be provided on a nonprofit basis? Unfortunately, experiences with this kind of facility have produced no definitive pattern that indicates which would be the most productive to serve travel needs. It really depends almost entirely on the efficiency of one individual—an individual who is just as likely to be found within the company as in an outside agency. The ability to set up complicated travel itineraries and to check and double-check reservations and time schedule changes in order to avoid any undue waste of travelers' time through foul-ups at terminals is the measure of success of any travel aid facility.

Security, as it relates to the individual in the office, is the second of this three-part subject. *Personnel security* is concerned with the safety of the employee insofar as the company can help it. For example, companies have arranged for two-way transportation between offices and major depots when the offices are in an out-of-the-way location or when much work is done at night with employees subjected to the possibility of being molested while going to and from work. In planning the office space, an effort should be made to locate all those who work at night as close to each other as possible and in an area easy to secure against intrusion by outsiders. When the after-hours work shift is long enough to require coffee breaks and/or meals, food should be made available on the premises.

Women employees often have wallets, change purses, and charge cards snatched from their handbags. The best way to avoid this, of course, is to insist that handbags be locked in desk drawers or carried whenever the handbag user leaves her desk.

Although more common in multiple-occupancy buildings than in single-company structures, robbery and molesting in restrooms is an unhappy fact of life today. Many companies insist that each employee "take a friend along" when going to the lounge.

However, purse snatching and robbery, the sale and use of narcotics, or other possible crimes are problems that beset society as a whole. They are not exclusively business office concerns. They certainly have no impact on space use and, unless they are neighborhood-related, are not the cause for relocation. They are mentioned here only to alert management to the fact that thought must be given to alleviate any of these problems that may be approaching serious proportions.

ENVIRONMENTAL CONSIDERATIONS

The environmental considerations that should be studied when planning for personnel include the determination of the basic concepts of space use (to be discussed in Chapter 7), the physical elements of lighting and acoustics, and the whole subject of design, which will add form, finish, and color to all that is being planned.

Design criteria, set up to meet company aims, will be described in Section IV, dealing with plan development. Concern here is for the impact of design on the individual. There was a time when flooring, fabrics, draperies, wall covers and, color were dictated by management usually through or for the designer. Choice, if given at all, was given only to the top echelon of management with each executive hiding personal "taste" behind the closed doors of a private office. The "democratic" process spread slowly but always within the sanctity of closed doors. The right was given to lower echelons of private office occupants to choose from a variety of colors, but all within a predetermined spectrum. The choice would be confined to the color of the particular carpet, chair fabric, or drapery fabric. In only rare instances was there a deviation permitted from an already chosen furniture style, although executives were occasionally allowed to choose their own desk chairs. Even that choice was usually limited to variations within a style.

Despite the rather minor increase in the number of people who are allowed some choice in the makeup of their particular environment, design is still very much a dictated part of office planning. The only real change that has taken place is the fact that the subject is discussed with more people. The need to design in terms of the individual, to give each person a greater sense of fulfillment, to be happier on the job and therefore more efficient at it, has influenced the design of the things each uses.

Chair dimensions (executive, stenographic, clerk, and visitor chairs) have all been modified (and in many cases made adjustable) for the benefit of the user. The same is true of desk dimensions, materials, and fittings as well as the color, finish, and practicality of files, cabinets, typewriters, calculators, and other equipment. This evolution in design thinking, applied also to colors, textures, and materials, has come about through the combined efforts of the designer (industrial and interior) and the behavioral scientist (ergonomist, psychologist, and physiologist) as they have applied their knowlege and skills to user needs.

Despite the progress made in designing for people, there are many persons whose working needs have been ignored or inadequately considered. If the company plans to give jobs to the physically handicapped, it must convey this fact to the architect, planner, and designer. To provide for the needs of the disabled adds no appreciable cost to the project, but it does call for advance planning. Door swings, pay phone heights, washroom facilities, and work stations are only a few of the things that have to be made accessible to and usable by handicapped persons. Information about the needs of the handicapped and how to meet those needs is abundant and available. Sources for this information are listed in Appendix 2.

SOCIOLOGICAL CONSIDERATIONS

Designing for people and planning for people are not "Johnny-come-lately" ideas. The wing chair was an eighteenth-century answer to drafty castles, while the Colosseum, designed nineteen centuries before the wing chair, handled its traffic problems so adroitly as to make a 747 green with envy. What is new is the emphasis being placed on the desire to provide for the individual as an individual and as a member of a work group. The whole planning process, as described in this book, is aimed at meeting organizational needs, operational needs, and personnel needs. It is only when personnel becomes personal that clarity dims a little. On all other matters, decisions were and will be made based on clear choices that lead to easily understood conclusions.

Planning and designing for the individual in order to answer the psychological needs of the office inhabitant are beset with problems that do not stem from a lack of desire to do something about them. Nor do they stem from a lack of ability to design for those needs. Management knows the importance of giving each worker a sense of fulfillment and knows that help is available to define the ways of providing it. The designer knows how to personalize individual "territory" and how to deal with the individual's needs in whatever role (creative, aggressive, cooperative) will provide the relationships that the individual wants to attain within the company. The problems are caused by the conflicts between the company's needs and the individual's needs and by the fact that the individual moves from one job to another, both in and outside the company. The conflicts can be solved only by compromise, and compromise can be intelligent only if the tools of compromise, the alternatives, are known.

The company needs are known. That is what the study of organization and operation is all about. Some of the individual needs are known: the tasks to be done, the required relationships of individuals to each other and to company services in the performance of those tasks, and the work station equipment necessary for that performance. Privacy needs, quiet concentration needs, physical environment needs, and security needs are already known. How these needs are all accommodated will be further studied as part of the analysis of layout concepts discussed in Chapter 7. What has not been studied, analyzed, and considered, or even thought about up to this point, is the individual as an individual, who has personal feelings, an individual behavior pattern, and a sense of personal dignity. What bearing do influences inside and outside the company have on an individual's behavior at work? Within the limitations of company goals, how do individuals achieve a sense of belonging, how can they improve their relationships with others, and how can they be provided with the status and recognition they need as individuals? And yet consideration of the individual, along with the desire or need for self-expression, for privacy, and for social contact, must be a matter of company policy to be determined at the time of planning. The behavioral scientist and the psychologist are available to help formulate policy or suggest policy for management's consideration.

Although the clichés that are associated with this whole subject, such as "human dignity," "sense of fulfillment," and "job enrichment," have been considered without a blush in this chapter, their use must not obscure or invalidate the importance of the problem. Because there is no simple answer, no easy solution, the need to deal with the problem should not be shrugged off. The final compromise between individual and company needs should be arrived at only after careful and serious deliberation.

7 Planning Space

It is important to realize at the outset that there is no one answer that will solve all space problems for all companies. The human factor, the ingrained work habits of company personnel and their capacity for change, must be as carefully weighed in considering alternative space concepts as they have been in considering possible changes in systems and procedures. In both instances the success or failure of the recommended changes will depend completely on how well the "producer" functions after the fact of change. A poorly run company will continue to be poorly run no matter how radical the change in space-planning concept. This truism is just as valid, in reverse, for a well-run company. The elements that should fall into place before new concepts can be considered must be (1) the establishment of the need for operational changes, (2) the fact that a different concept of space use will provide a better home for those changes, and (3) the responsibility of management to enforce those changes.

SPACE CONCEPTS

The basic concepts of space use fall roughly into these three categories: conventional or "closed" plan, modified conventional plan, and open plan. Study of each may indicate that some combination of all these concepts may be the most desirable. A comparative analysis should deal first with the operational efficiencies to be gained with each concept and the kind of personnel problems that would be involved in adopting one or another of them. The analysis should then include the amount of space each would require, the cost of the initial installation, and the cost of making a given percentage of space changes over a specific time period.

Extravagant claims have been made by proponents of each of the concepts. Landscape and open-plan advocates each claims to utilize less space as compared to the other concepts. Some conventional planning devotees claim that the other two concepts are fads and that the individual functions best in a private office and always will. All three claim to have the edge on the others when it comes to providing a good working environment. The best way to make an objective comparison is, of course, to ignore all claims and start from as unprejudiced a point as possible. That means that any preconceived ideas that management has must be ignored.

Also to help make the decision as unprejudiced as possible, the sociological factors of "work habits," "private office," and status syndromes have to be eliminated from the lists of advantages and disadvantages of the concepts that are part of the description of each. Instead these human factors should be understood as facts of life to be faced by management and treated independently from the concept chosen. No concept has a corner on the humanities market. How much consideration is given to the individual is a company decision, based on factors outside of any of the concepts. What this does emphasize is the need for a carefully planned and orchestrated orientation of company personnel, particularly when the concept to be adopted means radical changes in work patterns and work habits. The company that has kept its people informed all during the planning stages, whose personnel has participated in the studies of word processing, records management, and all other systems and procedure changes contemplated, will have a better grasp of the reasons for changes in planning approach. All aspects of and reasons for the changes should be explained as soon as the decision has been made to change. This should include indoctrination about the physical and operational changes as well as the advantageous sociological adjustments that the new concept will make necessary. If possible, the names of other companies working under the same concept of layout should be mentioned, and when available, pictures of their installations should be exhibited to company personnel. Also, if possible, administrative executives from those companies should be invited to talk at an orientation meeting.

It is no longer necessary to base plans on the geometric pattern forced upon companies in the days when it was impossible to get good ventilation except from an open window. This meant row upon row of offices separated from equally monotonous rows of offices by connecting corridors, all following the "U" or "L" or "W" shape of the only kind of building possible prior to air conditioning. In the main this caused an inefficient use of space and time-wasteful traffic patterns that had no relationship to the realistic needs of the organization.

It caused another problem, too, by getting people used to private offices. It fixed, in so many minds, the idea that the private office was a status symbol—at least it did so in the United States. But that idea is not universally ingrained; it changes from country to country. In Japan, for instance, the private office is almost nonexistent. It is reserved mainly for those charged with top-level responsibility, but even many in that category share an office with two or three other executives.

Ideally, therefore, a study should start with a thorough understanding of the principles behind each concept, the way in which each can be translated into a preliminary plan of space use, and finally, with an analysis of the costs for installation and maintenance. The recommendations to be made after the study has been completed will have to include a report on the human reaction to any change in concept and the ability of the company staff to work at peak efficiency within that concept.

The descriptions of the various concepts that follow are not necessarily in agreement with anyone else's definitions, nor is there any important reason why they should be. It is important that the similarities and the differences among the concepts and the possibility of combining two, or all three of them, be thoroughly understood. It is important to know, also, that any planning concept that is decided upon should be chosen not as a design solution but as a solution to the functional problems of the company whose space is being planned. Design must be the product of the concept, not vice versa. Done in proper chronological order, the decision concerning concept cannot therefore be made until all possible changes in systems and procedures have been decided upon. The lessons learned from the departmental and operational studies become the most important elements in the proper development of a valid plan.

The closed plan attempts to parallel the general outline of a company organization chart with size of office assigned according to importance of title. There can be as many as ten or more private office sizes and a variety of semiprivate offices to house two, three, or four people. Open areas or bull pens then house stenographers, clerks, and others who perform supporting functions.

Placement within the closed plan, if it follows the responsibility and communication lines of an organization chart, generally means that there will be an isolated executive area, clearly delineated departments, and service areas located so as to provide the best service to the most people. In some instances a top executive, with specific departmental responsibility, can be located in the department rather than in an executive area because of the importance of constant contact with department personnel. Also in large organizations, service departments may work better with satellite areas located throughout the company space. On the theory that one needs privacy to work efficiently, the conventional plan perpetuates protocol through privacy and size of space assigned, and by "awarding" the kind of furniture and furnishings commensurate with position.

The advantages of the closed concept are:

1. The plan can be adopted to any configuration of building shape and any floor size, both large and small.
2. Visual and accoustical privacy are assured.
3. Security is easy to maintain.

The disadvantages are:

1. The plan itself does not give employees a feeling of being part of the company, even if the company has an open-door policy.

2. Supervision is difficult.

3. Future layout changes will be both difficult and costly.

4. The hierarchical plan makes it difficult to follow a functional flow of work, particularly when paper and communications cut across departmental lines.

The modified conventional plan maintains those private offices that study indicates are essential for functional reasons, while everyone else is housed in open areas, in arranged rows of regimented work stations. Whether departmental delineations should be rigidly adhered to or not, and what kind of acknowledgement to hierarchical protocol should be made within the open spaces, is a decision of management. It is not dictated by the concept itself. For privacy and security reasons, conference rooms, meeting rooms, libraries, reception rooms, file rooms, and mail rooms should be walled in.

The advantages of the modified conventional plan are:

1. Departmental lines do not have to be maintained rigidly as in the closed plan, thus making it possible to follow to some extent, the actual operational flow.

2. A greater degree of flexibility makes physical changes easier to accomplish.

3. Security and privacy can both be maintained.

The disadvantages are:

1. The plan is not as readily adaptable to small or narrow spaces.
2. The individual is still restrained within organizational rigidities.

The open plan moves the entire company operation into open space, and by removing all individual department boundaries, permits planning to freely follow work flow. The only barriers to this free flow are those created when a company occupies many floors.

There are, according to the definitions prepared for this book, two types of open plan. In one, the layout of furniture and equipment follows the geometric patterns of the modified plan but uses a variety of work station systems and sizes that tend to minimize the regimented look. In the other, termed "office landscape," the work station units are arranged in groups, free of geometric patterns and separated from other groups and individual work areas by screens (both straight and arc-shaped) and plantings. The screens and plants provide visual limits for individual and group areas and also accord a fair amount of acoustical privacy.

In each of these concepts, which differ considerably in overall appearance and in the furniture and equipment needed to make each function, all echelons of personnel work together in open areas, abandoning all hierarchical elements of protocol and status.

The advantages of the open plan concepts are:

1. By eliminating departmental barriers the plan can conform to the functional flow of the company.

2. Communication among working units is simplified.

3. Plan changes become easy to accomplish and extremely inexpensive.

4. The lack of private offices adds to the individual's feeling of involvement with the organization.

5. Air conditioning is less expensive.

The disadvantages are:

1. It is most effective on large, open floors that are at least 50 to 60 ft wide and as column-free as possible.

2. New furniture and equipment are essential.

3. Acoustical control is far more critical in large, open areas and will therefore be more costly.

Despite all the advantages and disadvantages, no concept (closed, partly closed, open, landscape, or a combination of two or more) can be the right one until all the client's problems, both operational and human, have been thoroughly explored. Failure to make such a detailed, total exploration will mean the loss of opportunity to make exciting, meaningful changes in company operations. Once the needs have been explored and the decisions have been made about concept, management must insist on the permanency of the change and company staff must be trained to guard vigilantly against any plan deterioration despite the inevitable operational and organizational changes that will take place over the years. It would be criminal to have the landscape of today become the weed garden of tomorrow.

After the choice of a space concept has been made, the number of square feet that will be used must be resolved in order to proceed with an analysis of the housing alternatives. This resolution can only be made after space standards for all work efforts have been decided, all physical and structural requirements that have a bearing on space needs have been calculated, and predictions made of anticipated company growth from move-in date to a predetermined time in the future.

SPACE STANDARDS

"*Space standards*," or the number of square feet that a specific company will allot to work effort, include the sizes of private offices, individual work stations in open areas (and landscape areas), service areas, conference rooms and, in fact, any and all spaces required by a company for its operation. The actual allocation of space for any function should be a product of the need to fulfill that function. It is simple, for example, to do that for a word-processing task where the calculation becomes one of square feet for the equipment, square feet for the operator's movements, plus square feet for circulation to and around the work station. It becomes more complicated when one tries to determine the needs for an executive in either an enclosed private office or in a barriered space in an open plan. Does the executive see many customers who should be impressed by his or her status? Is a desk needed? Are files really needed? Is a comfortable seating area required? Should there be a private conference table or can a conference table be shared with others? Can . . . should . . . does . . . etc., etc., etc.? Each of these questions has to be answered for all the executives involved before standards can be fixed.

In fact, each of these questions has to be answered for everyone in the company. Space standards are actually a product of the work to be done, modified by the dimensions of the equipment required to do that work and by the intangible factor of individual or company status. In addition, the standards can be further modified by the plan concept to be used and by the module of the building, if there is one.

Figures 7-1 through 7-7 illustrate the minimum, unmodified space recommended for various categories of furniture and equipment as used in one or more situations. They are dimensioned to be of help when putting together a tabulation of requirements from which square-foot needs and furniture and equipment needs can be charted.

One other aspect of space use must be considered before it becomes possible to assemble all space needs into a tabulation of required feet. Although the subject of out-of-the-ordinary physical and structural requirements was touched upon briefly in Chapter 5, it is a good idea now to list all possible items in this category in order to calculate the impact of each on space needs.

The items most likely to require additional footage are those involving the piercing of a floor so that something or somebody can pass from one floor to the next. They include special elevators, dumbwaiters, shafts for cable, pneumatic tube conduits, shafts for conveyors of paper or other material, staircases, and escalators.

Special elevators are not those that will later be calculated as part of the building core, but elevators to be used for specific traffic between certain company areas. For example, for security reasons bond or cash elevators are used in some banks between processing departments and the bank vault. Also private elevators, for executive use only, are installed by some companies for reasons of protocol.

Dumbwaiters are often used to get supplies from the major supply area to the user area.

Staircases and escalators are used mainly as time-saving aids in multifloor installations and vary in size according to the reason for their installation. A back stairs, for employees' use only, will take far less space than a decorative stairs that goes from the main reception room to the executive floor.

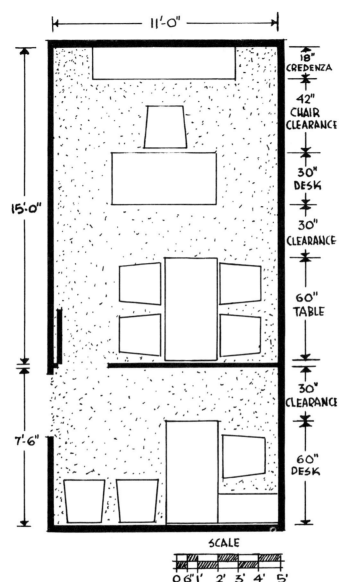

Figure 7-1
SPACE STANDARDS
Private Offices

11'-0"

18"
CREDENZA

42"
CHAIR
CLEARANCE

30"
DESK

30"
CLEARANCE

60"
TABLE

30"
CLEARANCE

60"
DESK

15'-0"

7'-6"

SCALE

0 6"1' 2' 3' 4' 5'

Closed-plan private office (minimum dimensions) with secretarial anteroom. The office group contains a credenza with file and storage area, a swivel chair, four conference chairs, a conference table, a secretarial desk, a posture chair, and two visitors' chairs.

Each of the other listed items is self-explanatory, and takes only the amount of space necessary for its proper functioning.

Other areas that may need structural consideration and require more space are photographic studios, display rooms, auditoriums, and screen rooms. Since some of these facilities, located in a standard office building, can require two stories to accommodate their need for height, the additional footage must be tabulated as part of the rent or building costs consideration.

Figure 7-2
SPACE STANDARDS
Private Offices

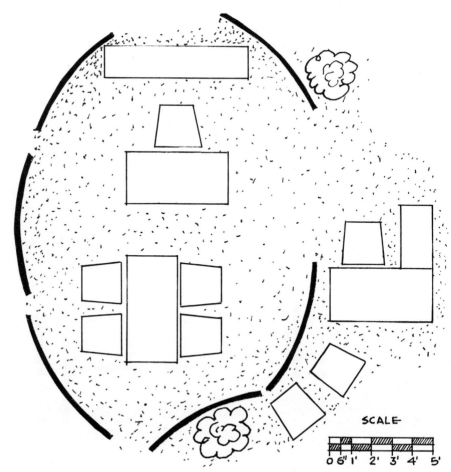

SCALE

0 6" 1' 2' 3' 4' 5'

Open-plan arrangement shows an office containing the same furniture and equipment illustrated in Figure 7-1.

Areas such as telephone equipment rooms or file rooms with a heavy concentration of file cabinets can, unless structural provision is made when the building is being constructed, require the spreading of weight load by means of surface placement of steel beams or steel plates. Such load spreading may require a larger area than would otherwise be allotted to house only the equipment or files.

PREDICTIONS FOR GROWTH

The last step, prior to tabulating the number of square feet required now, is to determine the number of years into the future for which space should be provided, the anticipated growth of the company over that span of years, and how many square feet of space that growth might require.

The number of years to be considered in the *prediction of growth* depends upon the manner in which the company is to be housed—in rented space or in a building of its

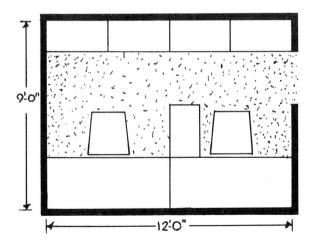

9'-0"

12'-0"

Figure 7-3
SPACE STANDARDS
Private Offices

Privacy in these two designs is attained through the use of self-contained work stations in which the partitions (at less than ceiling height) are part of the work station system.

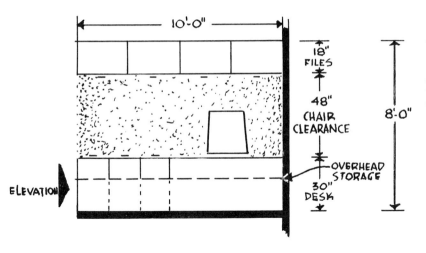

10'-0"

18" FILES

48" CHAIR CLEARANCE

8'-0"

OVERHEAD STORAGE

30" DESK

ELEVATION

These offices include many of the elements of furniture and equipment shown in Figures 7-1 and 7-2 (including the secretarial area). The conference space for this occupant would be in a shared conference/meeting room.

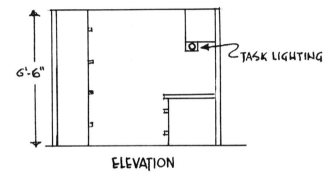

6'-6"

TASK LIGHTING

ELEVATION

Private area for one person. The elevation indicates one way in which task lighting can be installed in self-contained work stations.

Figure 7-4
SPACE STANDARDS
Desks and Tables

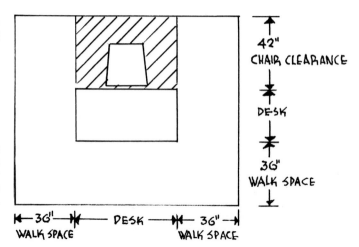

Single desk. Walk space may be in front and/or on one or both sides of the desk. Chair clearance should be no less than 36 in. and could go up to 48 in.

Single L-shaped desk. The "L" may be on either side with walk space in front and/or on one side of the desk.

own. If it is to be rented space, predictions should be made for at least 10 years into the future, and lease arrangements made according to the spread of square feet required over those years. It is not uncommon for a company to move into space that will be adequate for its needs during the first 3 to 5 years of its occupancy, maintaining options for the takeover of additional space in increments of 5 years for as long as the company anticipates staying in the space under lease and for as long a period as its predictions can be reasonably correct.

If ownership of a building is under consideration, valid predictions of company growth should cover as long a period of time as possible. Based on long-term predictions, companies have planned buildings twice as large as needed on move-in day and

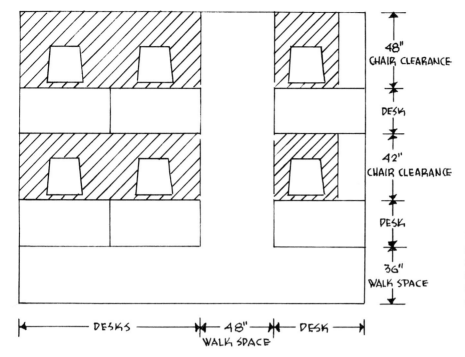

Figure 7-5
SPACE STANDARDS
Group of Desks

48"
CHAIR CLEARANCE

DESK

42"
CHAIR CLEARANCE

DESK

36"
WALK SPACE

Regular or L-shaped. The walk space between groups should range from 36 to 48 in., depending upon the amount of traffic. Chair clearance should also be from 36 to 48 in.

DESKS — 48" WALK SPACE — DESK

have subleased the unoccupied space on varying lease lengths. They then have been able gradually to take over that space for their own use, as needed. Should growth not be as rapid as predicted, the unused space can continue to be rented to others. In other cases, when there was no desire to become a landlord, the building was constructed to house the company for a predetermined number of years, with the plans drawn to allow for adding floors or wings to the original structure in order to take care of eventual growth. There are, of course, many other ways to plan a building for one's own needs without getting involved as a landlord, but that comes under the heading of real estate and will be discussed along with alternative ways of housing the company.

The actual predictions of growth, which should show anticipated growth by departmental units (departments, sections, or whatever component nomenclature is used) and service areas, can be made by in-house staff, or help can be obtained from an independent economic analyst. The growth of a company is activated not only by the desire of its executives and administrators, but to a great extent by socioeconomic factors over which the company has no control.

The development of data necessary for predicting growth can start with a year-by-year (or 5-year-by-5-year) analysis of company history. It should be charted, department by department, over as many years as the company records can supply the needed information about, and could include the total number of employees (in the past years) by department, the annual dollar volume of sales, the number of products produced, or the number of policies written (or whatever measure of company activity provides a

101

Figure 7-6
SPACE STANDARDS
Files and Shelves

Vertical files, "x" = walking/working space, which should vary from 1 ft 3 in. to 2 ft 3 in. for inactive files and should be 2 ft 3 in. for active files.

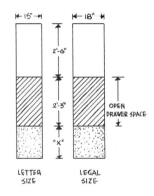

Lateral files. Walking/ working space should be the same as is required for vertical files. Lateral files come in three widths ("y")—30, 36, and 42 in.

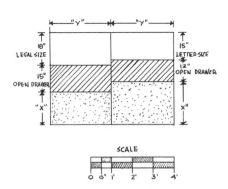

Open (shelf) filing. With no drawers to open, the walking/working space should be measured as above, but the measurements should be from the outer edge of the shelf.

All other files (plan files, card files, etc.) and shelves (storage, book, supply, etc.) are measured in the same way, with the walking/working space in front of each calculated according to the anticipated activity in that area.

If rows of files or shelves are placed facing each other in a file or storage room, the same calculations are used to determine walking/working space.

Note: The space required for banks of mobile, rotary, and automated files will be calculated, and room sizes determined, by the records management consultant or with help from the equipment manufacturer. The same should be true of space requirements for EDP, word processing, duplicating, and mailroom equipment, and for library equipment and furnishings.

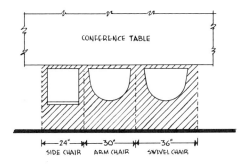

Figure 7-7
SPACE STANDARDS
Conference/Meeting Rooms

Passage space around the table should increase according to the number of people to be accommodated. If there are chalk boards, cork boards, or display rails at one end (or side) of the meeting room at which someone may have to stand, additional space of at least 3 ft must be provided to allow for movement. The same would be true if there is to be a speaker's podium in the room.

The rectangular conference table is acceptable for meetings of up to twenty people. Beyond that number, it loses its effectiveness since conferees are too far apart for easy communication. Wedge shapes, boat shapes, and rectangular tables in "U" arrangements should be considered for larger meetings. Classroom seating, with or without a conference table for major participants, is still another way to handle large groups.

Round tables can be very effective for meetings of twelve or less. Table sizes can range from 36 in. in diameter for four people, to 84 in. in diameter for twelve people.

Audio-visual consultants should be brought in to help work out room sizes for meetings where front or rear projection facilities are required.

consistent pattern). These data can then be compared (in chart form), in the same time span, to population changes in the areas served, gross national product changes, growth of the industry of which the company is a part, and the changes in percentage which the company holds in the total business of that industry. With the past charted, the graph can then reflect government and business associations' predictions in all those areas pertinent to the company's future, with the curves extended to show department and personnel growth necessary to accommodate that future. There then must be added to this extrapolation of statistical data such things as management's plan for increasing the company percentage of the total industry, the impact of any new products contemplated, or anything else that may be in management's plans for the future that would affect company growth.

Predictions, no matter how carefully worked out statistically, can be meaningless unless the study also includes an analysis of the general economy and a study of the

Figure 7-8　DEPARTMENTAL SPACE REQUIREMENTS

Department name: Accounting　　Department No.: 203　　　　　　　　　　　Date:

Title/Function	Space	Unit sq ft	19___ Units	Area	19___ + 4 Units	Area	Etc.
OFFICE SPACE							
Manager	PO	200	1	200	1	200	
Cashier & Ass't.	PO/2	300	1	300	1	300	
Ass't.	Same	100			1	100	
Subtotal—offices				500		600	
MISC. SPACE							
Files—letter	OA	8	10	80	12	96	
Cabinets	OA	15	2	30	2	30	
General work area—clerks	OA	80	7	560	8	640	
Storage—coats	St	20	2	40	2	40	
Storage—supplies	St	50	1	50	1	50	
Vault	V	90	1	90	1	90	
Subtotal—Misc.				850		946	
Subtotal—Department 203				1350		1546	
Intradepartmental Traffic—15%				203		231	
Subtotal				1553		1777	
Interdepartmental Traffic—10%				155		177	
Total—Department 203				1708		1954	

LEGEND:
　PO, private office; OA, open area; St, storage space; V, vault space.

Dep't. No.	Space needs				
	19____	19____ + 4	19____ + 8	Etc.	
101	12,700	13,800	14,000		
102	16,000	17,200	18,000		
103	14,000	15,500	18,000		
104	5,000	6,000	6,400		
105	22,100	22,300	22,600		
201	17,000	17,800	18,200		
202	15,400	16,900	19,000		
203	1,700	1,950	2,150		
301	22,000	23,100	23,200		
302	16,250	17,300			
503	18,000	19,000	19,800		
601	12,000	13,500	14,000		
602	5,000	5,100	5,400		
603	16,700	18,000	19,000		
604	8,000	8,700	9,000		
605	50,000	50,600	61,000		
Totals	650,000	680,000	720,000		

From these figures several decisions must be made: If space is to be rented, which year should be the determining one for the amount of space to be rented? How much space should be taken under an option or how much additional space should be taken immediately for short-term sublease to others?

If space is to be built, which year should be the determining one for the amount of space to be built? How much of it should be company-occupied at move-in and how much, if any, should be subleased for later take-back?

ability of the company's public to absorb any anticipated increase in "product." This means a study of changes in purchasing power, distribution methods, and the consumer mood for spending. The final results of these predictions can then be transferred to a table similar to that shown in Figure 1-2 or on a form similar to the one shown in Figure 7-8, which tabulates space requirements, department by department. Instead of showing a year-by-year growth, it can be done in whatever increments may be desirable.

SPACE NEEDS

In order to calculate the number of usable square feet that will be needed, 15 percent must be added to the total to provide for intradepartmental circulation and 10 percent to

Figure 7-10   DEPARTMENT REQUIREMENTS

Dept. No.	GROUPED BY SIZE: YEAR 19___ + 4						
	By Thousands of Square Feet						
	0–10	10–15	15–20	20–25	25–45	45–60	Over
101		*					
102			*				
103			*				
104	*						
105				*			
201			*				
202			*				
203	*						
301				*			
302			*				
503			*				
601		*					
602	*						
603			*				
.604	*						
605						*	
Recap	6	3	11	2	5	2	2

The department requirements, grouped by floor sizes, make it easier to see what basic sizes will best meet company needs. Two determinations were made after the study of the tabulations on Fig. 7-9. One was that the company would construct a building of 800,000 usable square feet, and the other that they would occupy 680,000 ft (19___ +4 predictions) at move-in. From this chart it was decided to build a base of five floors of 40,000 usable square feet and a 30 floor tower of 20,000 usable square feet on each floor.

provide for interdepartmental circulation. If the company is building for its own use, another 25 percent must eventually be added to accommodate the service core of the structure.

The square feet thus tabulated on the basis of the new space standards will be used to determine how best to house the company over the span of predicted years. Before trying to determine the ideal size and shape of the floors, it will be necessary to decide, from the tabulation of future footage, exactly what the target dates should be. For example, if the company is to move in the year 19___ should it, at the outset, provide enough space to take care of its needs until 19___ +3, or +4 or + 5, without having to take over any additional space? Also, should the company, renting or building, set its maximum space needs in the building to meet the requirements for the year 19___ or

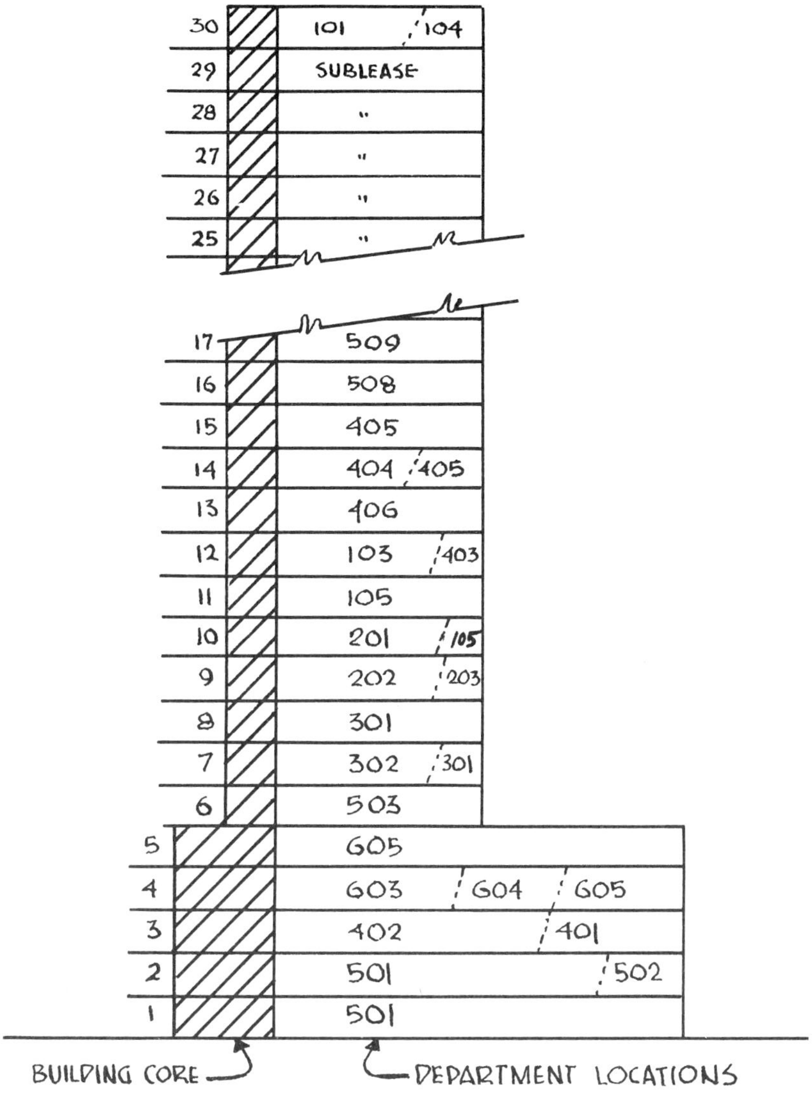

Figure 7-11
BUILDING PROFILE
Department Locations

Building profile (bottom to top):

Floor	Departments
30	101 / 104
29	SUBLEASE
28	"
27	"
26	"
25	"
17	509
16	508
15	405
14	404 / 405
13	406
12	103 / 403
11	105
10	201 / 105
9	202 / 203
8	301
7	302 / 301
6	503
5	605
4	603 / 604 / 605
3	402 / 401
2	501 / 502
1	501

BUILDING CORE · DEPARTMENT LOCATIONS

The profile shows the 40,000-sq ft (usable) floors that form the base of the building and the 20,000-sq ft floors of the tower. 25 percent has been added to each floor to take care of the building core.

The location of the departments would be determined by means of the traffic studies described in Chapter 4.

19_____? Once these targets have been set, both the initial and the final occupancy figures can be used to determine ideal floor sizes, ideal building profiles, the way in which space will be absorbed during the interim years, and the way in which the space concepts affect the floor-size decisions.

Figure 7-9 shows a department-by-department tabulation of space requirements. These requirements, grouped by sizes as shown in Figure 7-10, can then be used to determine the ideal sizes of floors to be rented or the size and shape of the building to be erected. Translated into the profile of an hypothetical building (Figure 7-11), it becomes possible to see how the departments and services areas would interrelate in a building.

Figure 7-12
FLOOR PLAN
Core Arrangement

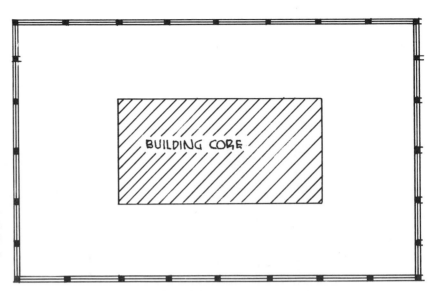

Centered core shows the 20,000 sq ft of floor space (+5000 sq ft of core area) as planned preliminarily.

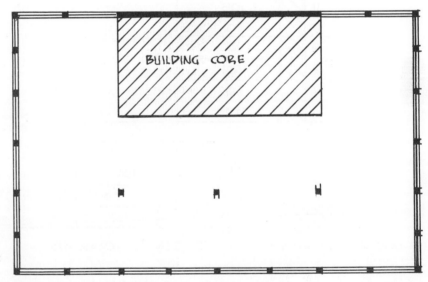

Offset core was prepared after test layouts of the various departments had been drawn. It shows the same floor and core areas with the core offset from the center to better accommodate department layouts.

The block layout of a floor (or floors) and the profile drawing through a building would be used in a search for a building (or space) to rent, or in the development of the ideal building to be constructed for company use.

Figure 7-12 shows a preliminary floor plan drawn for a new building. It also illustrates how that plan can be edited (before the building design is finalized) to provide space better suited to company needs.

Section II: Project Staffing

Before describing the talent required to carry out the project-planning efforts discussed in Section II, it might be best to avoid confusion and settle on some definitions. The three talents that need defining are:

Space Planner. As it is used in the book, the space planner represents that talent involved in analyzing the company operation, determining its needs, and planning the use of the space necessary to meet those needs. The space planner prepares all working drawings for the construction and installation of the interior space.

Architect. The architect designs the building (if there is to be a new one or an addition to an existing one) and plans it within the framework of the space needs program. The architect (with whatever engineering help is needed) determines the structural and mechanical systems for the building and prepares all construction documents necessary for bidding and building. For a more complete description of the role of the architect, see "Section III: Project Staffing."

Interior Designer. The interior designer designs the space, plans and selects the finishes, colors, materials, furnishings, and accessories, and selects all furniture and equipment except those items dictated by function.

All three of these talents can quite possibly be supplied by the same person or company. Each is available separately, and one or two might even be company staff. Each will be described separately in that section in which it is first used.

SPACE PLANNER

Except for the project manager and the project director, the space planner has the key role in any planning project. He (or she or they) becomes part of the project at the beginning to help with the feasibility study or after the feasibility study has demonstrated that a move is required. Once having started, the planner will be part of the job team until after the company has moved into the new space.

Space planners will conduct the inventory, the interviews with department heads, and the orientation meetings with management. They will work with the real estate consultant in the preparation of the lease and its work letter. They will coordinate their efforts with the architect (if there is one), with the structural and mechanical engineers, with those management consultants involved in systems and procedures studies, and with the interior designer in the study of aesthetic and environmental needs.

Space planners will also analyze the various planning concepts and prepare whatever plans are necessary to help explain to management the reasons for concept decisions. They will prepare recommendations for new space standards, determine the physical and structural requirements that will have a bearing on space needs, and help to prepare the tabulation of future space requirements. They will prepare all space studies and building profiles and help make the decisions about the housing alternatives. They will help prepare a budget estimate of all the costs involved in the project and prepare all the working drawings necessary for the bidding and building of all the approved elements of design and construction. They will secure bids when necessary, aid in the letting of contracts and purchase orders, and generally observe the progress of buildings and installation.

The fee of space planner consultants is expressed in a variety of ways. They all add up to the same basic concept, that of providing a profit to the planners after their time and their staff's time have been paid. The fee can be x number of cents per square foot, a percentage of cost, a flat fee of y dollars, a combination of cents per square foot plus a percentage of costs, time charges of personnel working on the job (usually billed as $2\frac{1}{2}$ or 3 times their payroll), or the lesser of the charges for staff time spent on the job against one of the first few methods. When the fee is so calculated, i.e., as time to a maximum, there should be a reward to the consultant of some percentage of the saved amount if the time charges are less than the maximum. In any event, fees from planners with equal credentials should be quite similar.

Possible sources for space planner talent include:

American Management Association
135 West 50th Street
New York, New York 10020

Contract
1515 Broadway
New York, New York 10036

Institute of Business Designers
1350 Avenue of the Americas
New York, New York 10019

Modern Office Procedures
614 Superior Avenue West
Cleveland, Ohio 44113

The Office
1200 Summer Street
Stamford, Connecticut 06904

Progressive Architecture
600 Summer Street
Stamford, Connecticut 06904

MANAGEMENT AND METHODS CONSULTANTS

The following consultants have all been placed under this one major heading because all are concerned, in one way or another, with changes in operational systems and procedures. No attempt is made to minimize the importance of any of the listed consultants although some will play more important roles than others, depending upon the needs of the specific project. Help of this kind should be obtained from independent sources with nothing to sell except advice. Fees, in all cases, should be based on the time spent by the consultant, restricted if possible to a maximum charge. As in the case of the space planner, there should be a reward for any savings against the maximum charge.

The work of each of the consultants listed below has already been described in Section II. It includes:

1. *Word processing*
2. *Records management*
   - Filing systems and equipment
   - Paper handling
   - Forms design
   - Duplication
   - Microfilming

3. *Supplies management and purchasing*
4. *Data processing*
5. *Communications*
- Telephone
- Intercommunications
- Facsimile (graphics communications)
- Audio-visual communications
6. *Service*
- Library
- Conference/meeting rooms
- Salesrooms
- Showrooms
- Security

Other specialized efforts already described in this section include:

7. *Medical*
8. *Food* (in-house dining)
9. *Recreation*
10. *Travel agency*
11. *Personnel security*
12. *Behavioral scientist*
13. *Psychologist*

Possible sources for the special talents listed above include (the numbers below are keyed to the numbers on the list):

Administrative Management Society
Maryland Road
Willow Grove, Pennsylvania 19090
1 through 6, 11

American Institute of Management
125 East 38th Street
New York, New York 10016
1 through 6

Food & Equipment Product News
347 Madison Avenue
New York, New York 10017
8

Institute for Professional Education
1901 North Fort Meyer Drive
Arlington, Virginia 22209
1, 2, 4, 12, 13

Institute of Management Consultants
347 Madison Avenue
New York, New York 10017
1 through 6, 11 through 13

Local medical society or hospital
7

Local universities and colleges with graduate programs in recreation
9

INTERIOR DESIGNER

The progress of the job to this point is such that neither the president's office nor the reception room is yet ready to be designed. Neither is it time to pick fabrics for draperies. It is time, however, to involve the interior designer, who will be responsible for the "look" of the space. He or she must attend all meetings covering "image," environmental and personnel considerations, space-planning concepts, space standards, and the preparation of the basic floor plans that will lead to the ideal size and shape of floor. What is eventually designed will be within the framework of each of those decisions and the designer must, therefore, take part in their making.

The interior designer will help in the preparation of the preliminary design budget. After it has been approved, he or she will select materials, finishes, and colors of all walls, floors, furniture, furnishings, accessories, and any other design elements. The interior designer will prepare all the drawings (colored renderings, black-and-white drawings, plans, etc.) and back-up material (photographs, samples, etc.) necessary to illustrate the design approach. Also prepared will be statements of all the costs and specifications necessary for the purchasing of design elements and all the details of design that must be included on the working drawings. Part of the job will be to expedite, if necessary, the delivery of those items selected and to supervise the installation of design, coordinating that installation with the construction and installation of the rest of the job. The interior designer's fee is usually based on a percentage of costs or on time charges.

Possible sources for interior design talent include:

American Society of Interior Designers
730 Fifth Avenue
New York, New York 10019

Contract
1515 Broadway
New York, New York 10036

Institute of Business Designers
1350 Avenue of the Americas
New York, New York 10019

Interior Design
150 East 58th Street
New York, New York 10022

MARKET RESEARCH/ECONOMIST

This consultant will help gather and interpret the data required when predicting company growth. Whether or not it is needed will depend upon the scope of the project, the length of time over which predictions are needed, and the capabilities of any in-house people to accomplish this. Possible sources for market research/economist talent include:

American Institute of Management
125 East 38th Street
New York, New York 10016

Society of Professional Management Consultants
205 West 89th Street
New York, New York 10024

Additional Efforts

Although not needed as yet for total involvement, the following might be required at this time for information only:

- *Real estate consultant*
- *General contractor or construction manager*
- *Legal advisor*
- *Architect*

III
Applying
the Plan

8 Renting

Preliminary work should have begun on the analysis of available options for housing the company while operational changes, growth patterns, and square-foot needs were being studied. The analysis should include a tabulation and study of property owned and/or leased by the company. The final real estate report should present recommendations for the use or disposal of these properties.

There are a number of specialists who can assist in such a study—consultants who will analyze plant and office relocation, firms who handle all the details of corporate personnel relocation, real estate consultants, and real estate brokers. Each of these specialties is described in "Project Staffing" at the end of this section.

LOCATION

In this study of choices the very first concern should be for the geographical *location:* Should the company stay in or close to its present location, or should the move be a major relocation to another city, another state, or another country?

Branch offices of advertising agencies, accounting firms, stock brokerage houses, service offices, and sales offices are located wherever they are needed to serve existing or potential clients. The focus of any location study for branch offices should, therefore, center on available buildings within a specific, almost predetermined, geographic area.

If it is to be a major corporate move based on corporate needs (consolidation of installations, a need to be close to clients' activities, or any one of a number of other reasons), the location study should encompass an analysis of work force availability and transportation facilities. Then, in connection with the alternatives of renting or building, relevant studies should be made of community problems, zoning problems, availability of housing for personnel, tax considerations, operating costs projections, and site studies. A site study should include the need for any required zoning changes and the possibility of getting them. It should also analyze roads (major highways as well as access roads), parking, utilities availability, and soil structure.

COMPARISON OF BUILDINGS

Whatever the decision, whether to rent or build in a new location or add to presently occupied space, it would be a good idea to know all the things that must be considered in the analysis of the choices. The study of this first alternative, to *rent space* in an existing building or in one already planned to be built, should start with a comparison of the buildings that might be considered in and around the agreed-upon location. Such a location should meet the requirements discussed in Chapter 1—the quality of the building, the proximity to an industry center if that is important, and the general quality of the neighborhood.

When comparing buildings, the basic building features should be studied and the availability of service required for company operation should be rated. If necessary, a comparison chart could be prepared to help the rating process and to help explain to management the reasons for the final recommendation. Figure 8-1 shows a sample of such a chart.

While an assessment is being made of these basic features, thought should be given not only to the adequacy of the facilities to meet immediate needs but also to their ability to accommodate foreseeable changes. Understand, however, that this should be only a comparison of basics—such things as basic air conditioning and basic electricity. The specific company requirements for things in excess of those usual to speculative office buildings are listed and described in that portion of this chapter dealing with lease negotiating.

On the assumption that the rent schedules are similar, the first area of comparison should be *floor size*. Can each of the buildings being considered house the company adequately, and will the size of the floors allow for efficiently planned space? Renting space usually means accommodating the requirements of the company in an existing or already planned building. It will therefore be necessary to edit the hypothetical profile that has been prepared. This should be done for each of the buildings under study and a rating ascribed to each building on an "adequacy" criterion.

Another area for comparison is *heating, ventilating, and air conditioning (HVAC)*. (This, and all the other basics to be discussed, is not placed in any order of importance.) A basic HVAC system should be able to provide inside temperatures of from 72 to 78°F

Figure 8-1 BUILDING COMPARISON CHART **119**
Renting

Item	Bldgs.			Remarks
	1	2	3	
HVAC				
Special exhausts (labs, kitchens)				
Electricity				
Elevators—passengers				
Elevators—service				
Escalators				
Stairs				
Material handling facilities				
Mail service				
Security systems—fire				
Security systems—theft				
Toilets				
Restrooms				
Floor loads				
Ceiling heights				
Underfloor ducts				
Emergency systems—electrical				
Emergency systems—elevators				
Loading docks				
Building maintenance crews				
Cleaning service				
Parking				
Newsstand				
Shops				
Basic work letter				

The only buildings that should be considered are those with adequately sized floors to house the company and with sufficient space available at both the desired move-in date and in the future to accommodate targeted growth. The items listed in the chart should be rated by letter or number. The last several blank lines provide space for comments concerning lease-negotiating efforts.

when the outside temperatures range from 0 to 95°F. Most systems are, or should be, designed to meet this criterion with an office occupancy of not more than one person per 100 sq ft of usable space and a standard electric load not in excess of 6 watts per square foot. Most buildings supply air conditioning from both peripheral units and interior machinery, with all air controlled thermostatically from central fan rooms. Each exposure of the building should be separately controlled from this fan room, thus dividing the building into four peripheral zones of air-conditioning control.

The building standard for *electricity* should provide for the delivery of all electrical energy to the space exclusive of that required for air conditioning. Most buildings will supply 6 watts of energy at 265/460 volts per sq ft of rentable area, of which 2 watts will be 120/208 volts. Electricity panels should provide at least 10 percent of spare circuit breakers for future requirements. Lighting fixtures, switches, and outlets for electricity, telephones, and other electrical requirements should be specified in the work-letter portion of the lease, to be discussed later.

Minimum *elevator* requirements are usually spelled out in local building codes. A rule of thumb for quickly judging the adequacy of elevatoring calls for at least one cab for every 50,000 sq ft of space when the building floor sizes are 50,000 sq ft or over. When the building floors are smaller, there should be one cab for every 35,000 sq ft. Also, no cab should serve more than twelve floors. However, there are other things to be considered when judging elevator adequacy. For example, if a company is using many small floors, requiring the use of more than one bank of elevators, this will pose traffic problems for personnel who try to get from one department to another. In fact, even if the floors are large, any required changeover from one bank of elevators to another has to be considered when analyzing personnel movement through company space. Also a study should be made of any traffic problems caused by the necessity to share elevators with other companies that have heavy interfloor movement.

Toilets are also a code-dictated facility, but rule of thumb indicates that in every 10,000 to 12,000 sq ft of space there should be three toilets and two washbasins for women and two toilets, two washbasins, and two urinals for men. If the company has many more women than men, or vice versa, will it be possible to enlarge one toilet room and make the other smaller? This should be explored and the building toilet facilities compared.

If the *height of the ceiling* is important to the plan, both slab and hung ceiling heights should be considered when the comparison of the buildings is made.

The *floor load* capacity must be considered if heavier than normal loads are anticipated in file, storage, or machinery areas.

In addition to judging these basic factors, note should be made in a building comparison analysis of any additional facilities that the buildings may have that could be important to the company. The following is a partial list of things to look for that might provide possible advantages for one building over another:

1. An under-the-floor duct system for electricity and telephones
2. Emergency generators for elevators, data processing, etc.
3. Escalators
4. Building security against fire and theft
5. Interior stairs and fire stairs
6. A newsstand
7. Shops
8. Loading docks and service elevators
9. Parking
10. Dead storage areas

Most office buildings throughout the United States have adopted the standard BOMA (Building Owners and Managers Association) method for *floor measurement*. This system for determining the rentable area of both multiple- and single-occupancy floors (see Figure 8-2) has been accepted and approved by the American National Standards Institute and is based on the premise that the area to be measured as rentable is that which the tenant may occupy and use for furnishings and people. In some cities floor measurements are computed so that there is a difference between rentable and usable square feet. To analyze rent schedules accurately, this difference must be known and used in comparing rents. Such information is readily available through the real estate consultant, the real estate broker, or the local real estate board.

The final step in building comparison, prior to entering into lease negotiations, is to test the floor plans of those buildings still being considered. This can be done by preparing space studies of typical company departments or service areas drawn on the building plans of those floors on which the departments might be domiciled. Studies of this kind will quickly show which building configuration best accommodates company needs and how effectively the desired plan concept fits within that configuration.

THE LEASE

The actual negotiation of a lease can be done by selecting the building with the best rating in the comparison "test." Arrangements should then be made for the company people and their specialists to meet with the owners and their representatives to work out a document satisfactory to all parties. Another way would be to have all the company specialists prepare a company version of a document (both lease and work letter) that includes all the things the company would like to get under the terms of the lease. This could be submitted to those owners whose buildings were still under consideration. The counter offers could then be studied, one building selected, and final negotiations concluded with that building's owner. Over the years the first method has

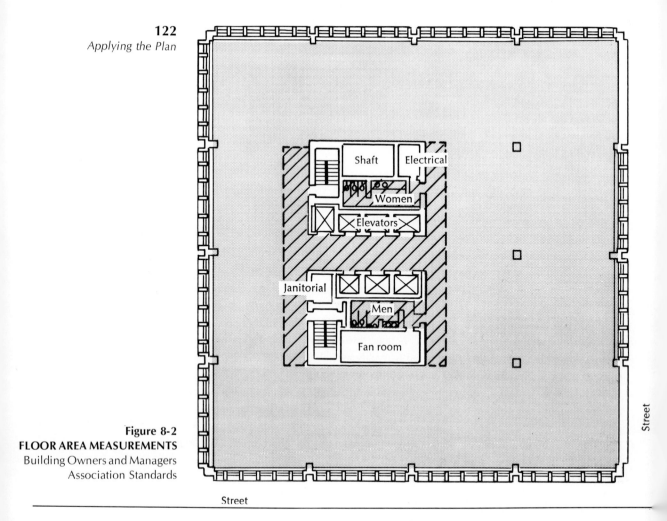

Street

Street

proved to be the more satisfactory. It is a faster way of accomplishing a desired end and usually makes for a better tenant/landlord relationship.

In connection with the feasibility study discussed in Section I, a preliminary cost estimate and analysis was made for the various housing possibilities. The cost analysis for renting was shown in Figure 2-3. That analysis should be constantly updated during the progress of the job. It would be well to start updating at this point in the study and keep all costs current as negotiations continue. Costs should, in fact, be kept up to date as the project effort continues into design, working drawings, purchasing, construction, and moving, not only as a guide to budgeting but as a constant check on expenditures.

The lease itself may be a voluminous document, particularly when a great amount of

Rentable Area

Single-Tenancy Floor   The rentable area (all of the shaded area on the illustration, p. 122), whether below grade or above, shall be computed by measuring to the inside finish of permanent outer building walls, or from the glass line where at least 50% of the outer building wall is glass. Rentable area shall include all area within outside walls, less stairs, elevator shafts, flues, pipe shafts, vertical ducts, air-conditioning rooms, fan rooms, janitorial closets, electrical closets—and other such rooms not actually available to the tenant for furnishings and personnel—and their enclosing walls. Toilet rooms within and exclusively serving only that floor shall be included in rentable area.

No deductions shall be made for columns and projections necessary to the building.

Multiple-Tenancy Floor   The net rentable area of a multiple-tenancy floor (all of the shaded area on the illustration, p. 122, minus the cross-hatched area within the dotted lines), whether above or below grade, shall be the sum of all rentable areas on that floor. The rentable area of an office on a multiple-tenancy floor shall be computed by measuring to the inside finish of permanent outer building walls, or to the glass line if at least 50% of the outer building wall is glass, to the office side of corridors and/or other permanent partitions, and to the center of the partitions that separate the premises from adjoining rentable areas.

No deductions shall be made for columns and projections necessary to the building.

---

space is involved. It consists of the "fine print" clauses of responsibilities of landlord and tenant. It spells out the rules and regulations that are usual in most leases, and the "dollar and cents" clauses that deal with such money subjects as rent, escalation, and options. It contains the work letter section that deals with the landlord and tenant obligations relative to the planning and construction of the tenant's space.

The legal and real estate advisors will help with the details of the "fine print" and the "dollar and cents" clauses. The major effort on the work letter will be that of the space planner and the construction manager or general contractor. However, neither one of them nor the author nor the publisher can substitute for the legal advisor. The practice of law should be left to him or her. The information in this chapter concerning the things that could be included in the lease is not an indication that professional help can be bypassed when dealing with the legalities of these documents.

The "dollar and cents" section not only will include rent and escalation but also should include anything concerning the future disposition of the space: (1) the right to sublet, (2) how any profit on sublet would be handled, (3) options for renewal and options on additional space, (4) the landlord's guarantee to the takeover of presently leased space, (5) the landlord's guarantee to rent space to others on short-term leases even though the company has included that space in its overall lease, and (6) the company's right to rent additional space within a specified time limit after planning begins.

There is another course of action that could make most of the "dollar and cents" and all the work letter parts of the lease extraneous. This would involve a "net lease" arrangement, whereby the company would lease the entire building and, in the process, take on the responsibility of maintaining it, operating it, and, if there were other tenants, keeping it rented. This possibility should be explored by the real estate consultant in both a renting and a building situation. Many times builders and developers will build a building to the company's specifications (with the company's choice of architects, planners, and designers) and then rent it to the company under this "net lease" plan. This can be a very satisfactory arrangement for both company and builder. In a similar plan, known as "sale, lease back," the company builds its own building, sells it to a third party, and then leases it back.

THE WORK LETTER

Usually when space is rented, it is the work letter portion of the lease that deals specifically with capital dollars to be spent or saved. It is this section that specifies the work to be done, who will pay for it, and what the landlord's and tenant's obligations are concerning this work. The end results should represent the realistic economic position of both tenant and landlord at the negotiating table, tempered by the landlord's need for the tenant or vice versa. What really makes the work letter important to the landlord and the tenant is that it should help to avoid future conflict. If it is carefully prepared to consider all possible contingencies, there should be no arguments about charges for completed work.

The first part (Part I) of the work letter deals with plans—those to be prepared by the tenant and those to be prepared by the landlord. Tenant's plans, as a rule, include the information for the construction and finishing of the space and the information required for the preparation of the engineering plans. This engineering information covers such things as unusual heat loads from equipment, electrical needs, plumbing requirements, air conditioning requirements, and weight loads. All this information should be included in the preparation of plans for structure, electricity, plumbing, heating, ventilating, and air-conditioning engineering. The landlord usually assumes the cost of

engineering plans and is responsible for the operation of structural and mechanical
systems. The structural and mechanical engineers who have planned the basic building
system will prepare the engineering plans to meet tenant requirements.

This section will also list the dates when plans must be submitted by the tenant to the
landlord. If many floors are involved, dates for the delivery of plans will usually be
staggered to meet the contractor's ability to prepare the floors for occupancy by a date
stipulated in the lease. Normally the first information required by the landlord will be
that which affects the structural and mechanical engineering plans. The last information
required will concern colors and finishes for painting and wall covering.

The responsibility for filing all plans, securing approval from jurisdictional authorities,
and paying all fees should be assigned in this part of the work letter. By agreement noted
in the work letter, tenant and landlord will conform to all local laws, rules, and
regulations.

The second part (Part II) of the work letter usually deals with the landlord's work, and
it is in this section that the items to be supplied by the landlord, above and beyond the
"building standard" items, are to be enumerated. (The term "building standard" is used
to cover those things offered by the building owner to all prospective tenants and
usually includes the basics of partitions, doors, hardware, lighting, outlets, switches, air
conditioning, flooring, ceilings, plumbing, and painting necessary to allow a tenant to
occupy the space being rented. The additional items agreed to in negotiation are then
added to the work letter within this section.)

The aim of any tenant is to get as many things included in this work letter as possible.
A list of such items should be prepared by all the specialists involved in space planning,
design, systems and procedures, construction, and real estate. All things studied in the
analysis outlined in Section II must be reviewed again to make certain that nothing has
been overlooked on the list of items to be negotiated. Finally the list should be prepared
and coordinated by the project manager and a dollar value ascribed to each item in
order to help the negotiating process. Which company people will participate in the
negotiation meeting is a decision that management will make, but it is of vital importance that both legal aid and the project manager be present at all sessions.

Work letters generally follow a rather standard format. The following several pages
show both the format and the general content of a fairly inclusive work letter starting
with Part II. The specifics would vary from one project to the next. Most items are self-
explanatory, but explanations where needed are given in italics and in parentheses.

This is not a sample of a work letter to be used as is. In repetition of what was said
before, the actual work letter, if it is to be an effective, dollar-saving bill of particulars,
will require the input of the space planner, the construction manager, the real estate
consultant, and, of course, the legal advisor.

Appendix to Chapter 8: Sample Work Letter

PART II: Landlord's Work Basic

In accordance with Tenant's Plans, Landlord, at Landlord's expense except as otherwise expressly specified in this Exhibit A and in the foregoing lease, will make and complete in and to the Demised Premises the following work and installations, all of which shall be of material, manufacture, design, capacity, finish, and color of the standad adopted by Landlord for the Building.

PARTITIONS, DOORS, AND HARDWARE

PARTITIONS

Furnish and install _____ lineal feet of ⅝-in. gypsum wallboard and 2½-in. metal stud partitions, spackled and taped for painting, with batt insulation to height of mechanically suspended ceiling.

   Furnish and install _____ lineal feet as above with two layers of ⅝-in. gypsum wallboard on one side of the partition erected from finished floor to the underside of the slab above.

(This is to prevent sound leaks through the ceiling area, from one office to another.)

   Furnish and install _____ lineal feet of Gypsum block partition plastered both sides for cafeteria, accounting vault, and jewelry vault; thickness of such block per Building Code.

Furnish and install, at a Work Cost not to exceed $____ per lineal foot, ____ lineal feet of all steel bankscreen partition, as manufactured by _____ or equal. No doors or gates to be required.

Furnish and install ____ lineal feet of full height all-glass metal partition for Data Processing room.

SOUND BAFFLES

Furnish and install sound baffles within peripheral air conditioning enclosures where dividing partitions between offices on periphery meet window mullions.

DOORS AND DOOR FRAMES

Furnish and install full height (not to exceed 8 ft 4½-in. high) fire retardant oak veneer door 3 feet wide with door frames of 16 gauge rolled steel with jambs reinforced to receive and retain templated hardware. There are to be ____ single doors and ____ pairs of double doors. Such oak doors to be as manufactured by _____ or equal. Except as specified hereafter in this Exhibit, there will be no additional hollow metal doors or bucks, except those doors and bucks already installed as part of base Building core.

Furnish and install ____ oak dutch doors, with plastic laminate shelf and mail-slot cut out for each door.

Landlord will allow $____ towards furnishing and installing ____ pairs of glazed doors with glass side lights, one at each end of elevator corridors.

Furnish and install the following special doors:

2 3-hour Diebold vault doors, one for jewelry vault and one for the accounting vault.

4 1-hour automatic fire doors, Class B with Underwriters label, with see-through aperture and electronic security access control.

1 Thermo-insulated door and frame for test lab constant temperature room.

HARDWARE

Furnish and install one and one-half pairs of butts per door, ____ doors to be supplied with lock sets. All latch and lock sets to be _____ or equal.

Furnish and install one concealed closer for every ____ rentable square feet. All doors without closers shall have door stops. Such closers to be _____ or equal.

CLOSETS

Furnish and install no more than ____ coat closets, 6 ft wide × 7 ft 0 in. high with two leaf sliding hollow metal doors, one chrome plated coat rod, and one paint grade wood hat shelf.

CEILINGS

Furnish and install a mineral fissured acoustical tile ¾-in. × 12 in. × 12 in., _____, or _____ or equal) concealed spline mechanically suspended ceiling in the Demised Premises.

FLOOR COVERINGS

Furnish and install ⅛ in. × 9 in. or ⅛ in. × 12 in. × 12 in. (at Tenant's option) vinyl asbestos tile _____ or equal, color to be selected by Tenant.

Furnish and install 2½-in. base strip, Tenant to select standard color and whether straight or cove, vinyl, or rubber.

Provide and install ____ square feet of raised floor (including all ramping) with vinyl asbestos tile floor finish. Such floor to be _____ or equal.

ELECTRIC

DISTRIBUTION SYSTEM

Furnish and install an underfloor cellular system, including header ducts, boots and connections, in all floors above the First floor. Said cellular system shall be a triple duct system (cells to be 3 in. in depth) with one cell activated for normal electrical wiring, one cell activated for low-tension wiring, and one unactivated cell. The spacing of the activated cells will generally be on 6-ft centers, subject, however, to the necessity to conform to Building conditions. The Building will contain wires, risers, conduits, feeders, and switchboards necessary to furnish any room or area of the Demised Premises with electric energy in an amount equal to 6 watts at 265/460 volts per square foot of usable floor area in the Demised Premises, of which 2 watts will be at 120/208 volts. 20% of the cover plates to be recessed to carpet height.

LIGHTING

Furnish and install one recessed fluorescent lighting fixture with acrylic lens and overlapping trim for every 60 sq ft of rentable area. Each fixture will be 2 ft × 4 ft or 2 ft × 2 ft in size at Tenant's option. Furnish and install the initial lamps for such fixtures.

Furnish and install no more than ____ incandescent down lights. Such fixtures shall be ____ or equal. Furnish and install the initial lamps for such fixtures.

RECEPTACLES, OUTLETS, AND SWITCHES

Furnish and install the following:

An adequate quantity of ceiling outlets and switches for the lighting fixtures specified including one (1) switch in each private office. If requested by Tenant's Architect Landlord will group switches for lighting in open areas.

____ double switches controlling split fixtures to provide two level lighting.

Install 120 volt duplex receptacles one per 100 sq ft of Rentable Area. Such duplex receptacles shall be located in partitions at Building Standard mounting height or in the peripheral enclosures at the prefabricated knock-outs or on the floor directly above such cells of the cellular sub-flooring as are activated for such receptacle use, all as specified on Tenant's Plans.

Provide special electrical requirements as follows:

Unless indicated, 20 and 30 amp separate circuit outlets shall be 120 or 120/208 volts single phase or three phase in accordance with final drawings.

(This would be a listing of special circuit requirements for data processing, cafeteria, laboratories, etc.)

Landlord will furnish and install a master control switch remotely located.

TELEPHONE INSTALLATIONS

Furnish and install one telephone outlet for every 120 sq ft of Rentable Area in the Demised Premises including necessary empty conduit, but excluding all wiring and outlets and conduit for separate intercom systems, call directors, or other such similar installations. Such outlets shall be located in partitions at Building Standard mounting height, or in the peripheral enclosures at the prefabricated knock-outs or in the floor directly above such cells of the cellular sub-flooring as are activated for such outlet use, all as shown by Tenant's Plans.

Provide and install master antenna on roof. Tenant to furnish and install cable and outlets from roof using slots in the floor of the core telephone rooms for such purposes. Landlord will provide junction boxes in partition with 1-in. empty conduit stubbed-up into hung ceiling above.

DRINKING FOUNTAINS

Rough, handle, and connect _____ semi-recessed drinking fountains per floor. Additional roughing not to exceed a total of _____ lineal feet per floor to plumbing source.

BLINDS

Furnish and install venetian blinds and metal venetian blind pockets for all windows of the premises.

AIR CONDITIONING

Furnish and install 2 peripheral air conditioning units at each 5-window bay. There will be one such unit in each private exterior office. The primary air for said peripheral unit shall be controlled thermostatically in the central fan room; each exposure of the Building will be separately controlled in the central fan room.

For said peripheral units, furnish and install one automatic water regulating valve for each 5-window bay, and one thermostat for every two 5-window bays, and not more than 8 additional thermostats per floor in the premises.

Interior space shall be served by a control system with individual floor reheat thermostatic controls.

The air conditioning system shall be capable of providing inside conditions of not more than 78°F dry bulb and 50% relative humidity with outside conditions of not more than 95°F dry bulb and 75°F wet bulb, except that as the outside temperature conditions vary the inside space conditions shall be maintained approximately as follows:

Outside conditions, dry bulb	Inside conditions, dry bulb
66–72°F	72°F ± 2°F, 30–50% RH
72–80°F	74°F ± 2°F, 35–50% RH
85–90°F	76°F ± 2°F, 35–50% RH
91–95°F	78°F ± 2°F, 35–50% RH

The system shall be capable of delivering not less than 0.35 cu ft/min of fresh air per usable square foot, and of maintaining a minimum temperature throughout the premises of 72°F dry bulb when the outside temperature is 0°F dry bulb.

All of the foregoing design conditions specified above are based upon an occupancy of not more than one person per 100 sq ft of usable floor area in the premises, and upon a combined lighting and standard electrical load not to exceed 6 watts per sq ft of usable floor area in the premises.

Provide the necessary supply of air and furnish and install necessary reheat coils, thermostatic controls, and exhausting for ____ special rooms exclusive of Data Processing, Medical Department, laboratories, and cafeteria. Such special rooms shall not exceed _____ square feet each and shall not exceed a personnel capacity of more than _____ people each. Such special rooms are to be so located as not to exceed ____ special rooms per floor.

Allow $____ towards the cost of providing separate exhaust systems for laboratories, including five for dryers, one for three flamability testers, one for drycleaning machine, and one for high concentration heat generation equipment.

PAINTING

Paint such walls, partitions, columns, peripheral air conditioning enclosures, doors, door frames, and metal trim as are Building Standard. Such painting, in the case of non-metal surfaces, shall consist of one coat of primer and two finish coats of flat or semi-gloss paint, at Tenant's option, and a stippled finish and, in the case of metal surfaces, shall consist of an enamel undercoat and an enamel finish coat. Colors shall be selected by Tenant with no limit on the number of colors in any room or area.

Provide and install ____ lineal feet of vinyl wall covering to be selected by tenant. Cost of such wall covering not to exceed ____ per square yard.

PLUMBING

Furnish and install the following:

MEDICAL DEPARTMENT

Toilet in the Medical Department consisting of a sink, water closet, medicine cabinet, and recessed paper towel dispenser and waste receptacle. Roughing for above shall not exceed 10 lineal feet to plumbing source.

EXECUTIVE PANTRY

Allow $____ towards furnishing and installing a complete executive pantry to include (i) 30 lineal feet of plastic laminated counter tops, (ii) baked enamel steel base and overhead wall cabinets equal to ____, (iii) double stainless steel sink _____, (iv) four burner counter top range with double oven, (v) 22 cu ft refrigerator-freezer with ice maker, (vi) dishwasher, _____.

EXECUTIVE TOILET

Furnish and install one executive toilet to include water closet, sink, shower, medicine cabinet, and ceramic tile floor and walls. Roughing shall not exceed 10 lineal feet to plumbing source.

MISCELLANEOUS

Provide and install floor reinforcement not to exceed a total of ____ feet of floor area. Such floor reinforcement shall not increase the floor load capacity of the areas so to be reinforced to more than 100 pounds per square foot. Tenant agrees that the locations of the areas so to be reinforced shall be subject to the reasonable approval of Landlord.

Provide shaft for Vertical Conveyor carrying 20. in. $\times$ 16½ in. $\times$ 12 in. high trays. Location of such shaft as per reasonable approval of Landlord and attached sketch to this Exhibit.

Perform all engineering in connection with the work and installation specified herein.

PART III: Additional Work to Prepare Building

Landlord will provide a new freight and loading area. Such loading area will be located as per attached drawing.

Landlord will furnish and install two (2) 32-in. wide escalators from Concourse to 1st Sub-Level, in approximate location and dimensions as per attached drawing.

These escalators will be equal in design and manufacture to existing escalators from Lobby to Concourse.

Landlord will provide all necessary structural framing for such escalators.

Landlord will furnish, install, and maintain an emergency lighting system for the Building stairwells.

PART IV: New Materials, Additional Work and Additional Materials

As respects any item of work provided for in Part II of this Exhibit with respect to which a dollar allowance is specified or with respect to which the cost to Landlord of finishing such item is limited, Tenant shall pay Landlord the amount by which the Work Cost of such item exceeds the amount of the allowance or cost hereto so specified.

Tenant may select different new materials (hereinafter "new materials"), except venetian blinds, in place of Building Standard materials which would otherwise be initially furnished and installed by Landlord under the provisions of this Exhibit and the foregoing lease, provided such selection is indicated on Tenant's Plans and approved by Landlord. If Tenant shall make any such selection, or if new materials are required because of any situation created by Tenant, by reason of subleasing or any other cause, wherein the Building Code prohibits the use of Landlord's Building Standard materials, and if the Work Cost of such new materials shall exceed the Landlord's Cost of Landlord's Building Standard materials thereby replaced, Tenant shall pay to Landlord, as hereinafter provided, the difference between the Work Cost of such new materials and the Landlord's Cost of Landlord's Building Standard materials thereby replaced. Tenant may also indicate on Tenant's Plans, subject to approval by Landlord, additional work and additional materials to be furnished and installed by Landlord at Tenant's expense, and Tenant shall pay to Landlord, as hereinafter provided, the Work Cost of such additional work and additional materials. No new materials shall be furnished or installed in replacement for any of Landlord's Building Standard materials nor shall any additional work or additional materials be furnished or installed until Landlord shall have advised Tenant in writing of, and Landlord and Tenant shall have agreed in writing, on the Work Cost of such new materials and the Landlord's Cost of such replaced Landlord's Building Standard materials, or the Work Cost of such additional work or additional materials, as the case may be. All amounts payable by Tenant to Landlord pursuant to this Exhibit shall be paid by Tenant promptly after the rendering of bills therefor by Landlord to Tenant, it being understood and agreed that such bills may be rendered during the progress of the performance of the work and/or the furnishing or installation of the materials to which such bills relate. Any new materials and/or additional work and/or additional materials shall, upon installation, become the property of Landlord and shall be surrendered by Tenant to Landlord at the end or other expiration of the term of the foregoing lease. No credit shall be granted for the omission of Landlord's Building Standard materials where no replacement in kind is made. Any selection of new materials and/or additional work and/or additonal materials by Tenant is referred to as "special work" in the foregoing Lease. Tenant may elect to purchase its own carpet instead of using Building Standard vinyl asbestos. Credit for vinyl asbestos will be 30 cents per square foot up to 75% of the total rentable floor area.

The term "Work Cost" as used in this Exhibit shall mean the estimated or actual cost (including the cost of applicable insurance premiums and the cost of additional engineering, if any, required by reason of section _____ hereof) to Landlord of furnishing and/or installing new materials or additional work or additional materials, plus ____% of the estimated or actual cost (including the cost of applicable insurance premiums and the cost of any such additional engineering).

Unit prices on all items to be provided and/or installed are to be made part of this work letter. The term "Landlord's Cost" as used in this Exhibit shall mean the estimated or actual cost (including the cost of applicable insurance premiums) to Landlord of furnishing and/or installing Landlord's Building Standard materials thereby replaced. Tenant will have the right to purchase items of furnishings such as carpeting, drapery, etc., without Landlord's participation and involvement.

PART V: Tenant's Credit

Landlord agrees to allow Tenant a credit in the amount of $____ against amounts payable to Landlord pursuant to Part IV of this Exhibit.

The following Unit Prices are those in effect on _____ and are subject to escalation in accordance with contracts of the individual trades.

(These are samples of the kind of unit prices that, if applicable, should be made part of the work letter. Many more items may be included.)

A. Drywall:

    1. 2½-in. metal stud, 1 layer ⅝-in sheetrock each side to ceiling only; no insulation . . . . $ per LF

    2. Bldg. Std., 1 side to slab, 1 side to black iron, insulation to black iron . . . . per LF

    3. Same as item 2, plus additional layer to slab . . . . per LF

B. Masonry Partitions (including plaster finish):

    1. 4-in. hollow gypsum block w/plaster (2 sides) . . . . per SF

    2. 3-in. hollow gypsum block w/plaster (2 sides) . . . . per SF

C. Hollow Metal Doors (furnished and installed):

    1. Bldg. Std. 3 ft × 7 ft, including frame and hardware application . . . . ea.

    2. Same as item 1, 8 ft 6 in. high . . . . ea.

    3. Pair Bldg. Std. 6 ft × 7 ft . . . . ea.

    4. Pair Bldg. Std. 5 ft × 7 ft . . . . ea.

    5. Trimmed openings . . . . ea.

D. Closets (Bldg. Std.):

    1. 5 ft wide × 7 ft high . . . . ea.

    2. 6 ft wide × 7 ft high . . . . ea.

E. Hardware (Bldg. Std., furnished only):

    1. Latchset . . . . ea.

    2. Lockset . . . . ea.

    3. Butts . . . . per set

    4. Surface-high mounted closer . . . . ea.

F. Drinking Fountains:

    1. Semi-recessed, within 10 ft of wet column: Furnish, rough handle and connect . . . . ea.

G. HVAC:

    1. Additional peripheral thermostats . . . . ea.

    2. Reheat coil to 2000 CFM . . . . ea.

    3. Reheat coil—over 2000 CFM . . . . ea.

H.   Electrical:

    1. Furnish & install 15-A separate circuit device, wall-mtd . . . . ea.

    2. Furnish & install 20-A separate circuit device, wall-mtd . . . . ea.

    3. Furnish & install ceiling outlets, 1 or 2 fixt . . . . ea.

    4. Furnish & install ceiling outlets, 3 or 4 fixt . . . . ea.

    5. Furnish 2 × 4 ft B.S. recessed fixt . . . . ea.

    6. Furnish 2 × 2 ft B.S. recessed fixt . . . . ea.

    7. Furnish & install 3-way switch . . . . ea.

        etc.

There are other subjects that could be made part of the work letter. Each should be included only if it is essential that the subject be covered in great detail. One such subject is *fire safety*. The work letter could specify the building fire-protection system and control procedures that would assure the tenant of control against fire propagation, spreading, and damage and provide for occupant evacuation safeguards. The same kind of specifics could be detailed when treating the subject of *security*. The kind of guard protection, required sign-out procedures for all packages taken from the building, sign-in and sign-out rules for personnel, TV camera surveillance, and any other systems required by law or offered by the building should be added to the work letter. In addition (particularly when a great amount of space is being considered), it would not be unusual to have *cleaning specifications* listed in detail. These would include general items such as waxing, dusting, ashtray cleaning, and vacuuming. The specifications could also detail cleaning of lavatories, lobby, and other public areas, high dusting (pictures, lighting fixtures, etc.), window cleaning, porter service, and the bonding of cleaning personnel.

The project manager, in the role of coordinator, will compile the details of the work letter from information supplied by the space planner, records management specialist, communications expert, and other specialists. Prior to lease signing, with this information, the project manager can update the budgets for this project according to those items that were or were not included under the work letter terms. Once the lease is signed or the intent to sign it indicated, he or she can, with management's approval of the budgeted expenditures, set the wheels in motion for the preparation of the design and the construction drawing phases of project effort. Also the project manager can update all schedules for the purchasing and construction phases and target installation and move-in dates more accurately.

The preparation for all this effort starts with the finalization of the space study. Earlier, when comparing buildings, test studies were done of typical departments. With the space to be rented determined, space studies must be made of each floor to be occupied—studies that clearly indicate how and where each service area, private office, and open area is to be located. Although there must be space for each person, work station, piece of furniture, or floor-space-occupying equipment, none of these need be shown in the study. In fact, at this stage of plan development, it would be best not to get too detailed in the space study. The purpose of this study is to make it easier to grasp the overall relationships that are being established in the total company space and easier to understand how the approved changes in systems and procedures have affected company operation. This, after all, is the first opportunity to see how the new records management system helps to determine the distribution of file areas, how the introduction of word processing has changed the number and location of clerk typists and secretaries, and what impact satellite service centers have on layout. The details of placement of people and furniture and equipment, and even the size and shape of some areas, will be further defined and refined after the space studies have been approved and the project moves into its next phases—the preparation of design and working drawings.

9 Building

SINGLE OR MULTIPLE OCCUPANCY; EXTENSIONS TO EXISTING FACILITIES

The second possibility mentioned in Chapter 8, building for the company's own use, can be accomplished in one of three ways: by constructing a single-occupancy facility, a multiple-occupancy facility, or an extension to or near an existing facility. The existing facility could be a presently owned office building, a warehouse, or a plant.

Fortunately, the factors that can affect the choice can be defined:

1. To build near or add onto an existing facility requires that there be such a facility, that there is sufficient property available for building next to it or on it, and that the site can still meet all the requirements for location that would make it a desirable place for the company building.

2. To build a multiple-occupancy building requires that the company is willing to be a landlord.

3. If the answer to the first two possibilities is "no," there is no choice but to build a single-occupancy building and either have it built to specifications under the "net lease" arrangement described in Chapter 8 or build it to specifications and then sell it and lease it back from the new owner. These options should be explored by the real estate consultant.

Whatever the decision, an analysis of the building choice starts with a study of location. Once again the first question is, Where is this relocation to be accomplished?

Is it to be in or near the present location, or is it to be a major move to another city, another state, or another country? All the things concerning location that were considered when an analysis of renting was made must also be considered when building. This time, however, in addition to analyzing such things as work force availability, transportation facilities, and community problems, a major part of the analysis must be centered on the site itself.

Once zoning has been cleared for office building use, and the area height limitations are considered acceptable, careful study must be made of the physical quality of the site and its ability to support the building or buildings to be planned. A very careful study must be made (particularly if the location is to be outside of center city) of the network of roads that lead into the vicinity of the proposed building and the problems attendant to creating access roads to the site. Also, will the community be helpful? For example, will the local governing body pay for building and maintaining these access roads?

When exploring the possibility of community help, such exploration should include a complete analysis of local tax structures (real estate, corporate, individual, and others) and whatever concessions the local governing body may be willing to make to entice the company to locate in that particular area. Cities or states have been known to give very generous tax concessions to companies that build within their limits. In some instances, they have underwritten the salaries of newly employed local people because they would be given on-the-job training for skills they did not have. Help from the community, although not always available, is certainly worth exploring.

The size and shape of the building, the floor sizes and, in fact, the actual number of buildings become the design product of all the elements that have brought about the need for building in the first place, i.e., the number of square feet required, the size and relationships of departments, the people and material traffic, location, etc. But sometimes the size and shape of the building and its location are determined for a totally different reason—public relations. The form and finish of each building and the way in which each has made dramatic use of the plot on which it stands make Lever House and the Seagram's Building models of effective public relations on New York's Park Avenue. The Sears Tower in Chicago was designed as the tallest building in the world for no other reason than public relations. When a Canadian manufacturing company decided to construct a building of its own, there were many choices open to the company for building on its plant property. The building could have been placed along a major highway, with simple access roads leading to and from it, or it could have been placed completely out of sight, away from the road. The company chose to take advantage of some of the exciting manufacturing procedures that were open to the view of people going through their property. They placed the structure so that visitors would have to pass these sights on their way to the office building, which was designed and positioned so that it could also be seen, and admired, from the heavily trafficked highway.

One other consideration is the number of buildings to be built: should there be one building, or are the location and the operational requirements such that a campus arrangement of buildings might be more desirable? If a campus layout is the best solution, then the planning has to be horizontal as well as vertical, and such things as communication, transportation, materials handling, personnel traffic, and central services must be reexamined. If the departments are logically separable into three divisions, each housed in its own building, should a fourth building be planned as a heating, ventilating, and power plant or should the power plant be designed into one of the three buildings? Will people go from one building to another by walking or by mechanical means? If they are to walk, will covered walks be provided to protect them from the elements or should the walkways be underground, connecting passages that can serve also for the distribution of mail and supplies? Although the answers may be different, most of the questions asked are the same ones that have to be answered whether the company is to occupy one building or several buildings. Relatively few of the questions are peculiar to the campus plan, and those that are concern mainly the movement of people, material, and power on, over, or under the space between buildings.

The actual size of the building, the required square feet necessary to house the company plus 25 percent of that total for the core of the building itself, should now be shaped, in preliminary fashion, to conform as closely as possible to the previously planned profile of a hypothetical building. From here on, planning must be an accommodation of this ideal to the reality of the planning and building process and to the dollars budgeted in the first feasibility study analysis (Figure 2-3).

Now is the time to decide whether to plan a multiple-occupancy building and to analyze the reasons for doing so. If the additional tenant space is to be provided in order to make a profit on the real estate investment, the cost of the building (and its design features) may have to be edited to bring the rent in line with the local rental market. This aspect of the project should be carefully analyzed by the real estate consultant before proceeding with final plans. If, on the other hand, the additional tenant space is planned solely for eventual takeover by the company so that, someday, the building will become a single-occupancy structure, then costs need not be related to the rental market. In this event, the logistics of gradually taking over the entire building will have to be carefully planned in advance so that this takeover may be accomplished at the lowest possible cost and with the least possible disruption to the company operation. Also, the length of the tenant leases will have to conform to the pattern of predicted company growth and space needs.

STRUCTURAL AND MECHANICAL SYSTEMS

Starting at this point the efforts of the architect, space planner, interior designer, structural and mechanical engineers, and all the other specialists whose project input will have an impact on physical planning must be coordinated by the project manager. Unlike the planning done for rented space, many things that would not be included in a speculative office building can be made part of the company's own building. The plans of the building should include as "built-ins" whatever facilities or amenities are required to meet present and future operational, organizational, and building needs. These include conveyor shafts for materials and paper handling, vacuum systems for building maintenance, under-floor ducts, utilities to take care of steam, gas, or unusual water needs, systems for security and fire protection including sprinklers, closed circuit TV cables, paging systems, music amplification, and all the other things required or desired as a result of the studies described in Sections I and II.

In addition, planning a new building means the possible inclusion of a number of new factors and the necessity to make decisions based on each of them. The major contributors to this aspect of the project will be the architect, the structural engineer, and the mechanical engineer, all of whom will be guided by the project manager, who must make certain that all known company needs are provided for in the new building.

As part of the building design, the structural system and the mechanical system must be developed to consider such things as

- Floor loads
- Floor heights
- Elevators (passenger and freight)
- Escalators
- Stairways
- Loading docks
- Toilets
- Other water services
- Mail chutes
- Maintenance systems
- Emergency power and lighting systems
- Emergency ventilation
- Special exhaust systems

and all the things that were discussed in Chapter 8 in connection with renting space.

Many of the building components are mandated by local laws or building codes, while others must meet code specifications for performance and/or installation. There are New York City laws, for instance, that concern fire safety. They apply to all buildings over 100 ft in height and require that each building have a fire director, wardens, and periodic fire drills. They must have fire alarm and communication systems and either stair pressurization and floor compartmentation or a sprinkler system. Also elevators must be so controlled that they can all be immediately brought to the lobby in case of fire. The architects and engineers will be familiar with all these requirements and should provide management with a checklist of all mandated installations.

Lighting, accoustics, and power sources from floors and ceilings all require design analysis, so that in one way or another, they are given proper consideration when the building is being planned. Many of the items listed here should be treated as design elements, and the final decision concerning them should be postponed until the interior designer has completed the total design study of the space. That does not mean that the final decision will be the designer's; it does mean that design recommendations should play an important part in the decision-making process.

Thought must be given, also, to the peculiarities of the locality on the systems being designed. For example, if an area is subject to occasional water shortages, water should not be used as the only cooling source for the air-conditioning system.

INTERIOR STANDARDS

Along with the preliminary development of the structural system and the floor plans, a decision must be made concerning the modular system that may be used for all interior planning. The module, or building standard dimension, is usually dictated by the window size (or vice versa) and is carried throughout as a standard dimension for both peripheral and interior space. The most usual of such modules is 5 ft × 5 ft, but buildings have been planned on 3 ft × 3 ft to 6 ft × 6 ft modules including all the 6-in variations between 3 and 6 ft. Tests, in the form of space study plans, should be made to analyze the comparative space-saving effectiveness of one module against another. The module to be used would be a product of that test, modified, if necessary, to accommodate any desired elements of building design. The one thing that should be kept in mind is that no unusual sizes of ceiling tile, floor tile, or partition panel should be used as standard unless there is a very, very good reason for specifying other than the normal standard sizes. Wherever and whenever unusual sizes have been used, there have been unnecessary supply problems. The company has been forced to stockpile large quantities of the odd-sized material and to pay rent for its storage.

Once the preliminary plans have been completed, they must be tested through the development of space studies. The preparation of such studies was described in Chapter 8. After the studies have been approved by management, the project will move into the next phase—the final design of the building and of the interior spaces.

10 Renovation or Redecoration

The remaining alternatives to accommodate change are bracketed only because each is accomplished within the space already occupied by the company. Consideration may have to be given, in one or both of the choices, to the condition of the building itself and to the possible costs for its modernization. The electrical system must be inspected, with such things as wiring, panel boxes, emergency systems and lighting fixtures checked thoroughly. Elevators must be tested and overhauled or replaced if necessary. The heating, ventilating and air-conditioning system, toilets, basins, sinks, urinals, and all plumbing fixtures and pipes must be checked. The lobby and all public areas on tenant floors may have to be modernized, windows repaired or replaced, the facade of the building cleaned, and all ornamental metal and metal trim cleaned and polished.

SPACE RENOVATION

Renovation, as it was defined earlier, means replanning the existing space to accommodate all the desired operational and organizational changes and, at the same time, redesigning the space. Planning for renovation can be almost as involved in details as planning for renting or building. While it eliminates the need for location search, site studies, personnel moving, and the other details that are part of relocation, it does have the added complication of trying to build space within which the day-to-day operations of a business are being conducted. It thus adds a cost not easily measurable in dollars.

Renovation also means that part or all of the existing facilities (partitions, lighting fixtures, ceilings, etc.) must be demolished, and that, in turn, means that the measurable costs for renovation are often greater than they would be for the construction of new, open, and unoccupied space.

The first order of business, if the existing space is rented rather than owned, must be an examination of the lease commitments. Is the present lease of sufficient length to warrant the renovation expenditures or should the lease be renegotiated before getting too far into the planning stages? If the lease is to be renegotiated, is the renting situation in the building and in the locality around the building such that it may be possible to include a work letter in the lease to list the things the landlord may supply under the lease? Very definitely, an opinion should be sought from a real estate specialist, whose help should also be used in negotiating, if negotiation is possible. The project manager should prepare a specific list of items that may be part of the work letter. The preparation of the work letter was described in detail in Chapter 8.

But, whether the lease is renegotiated or not, once it has been decided to renovate, the next step in the project should be the preparation and finalization of the space study. The study should reflect all the procedural and operational changes agreed to earlier and should prove to everyone's satisfaction that the renovated space can accommodate the company. It should also show the basic amount of demolition and reconstruction that will have to be done. (It can, in fact, help to determine many of the items that may be made part of the work letter.) Once approved, the study becomes the starting point for the rest of the work to be accomplished, including the design and working drawings for bidding and building the space.

When the decision to renovate was first made, it was based, in part, on the budget estimate of costs prepared with the first feasibility study. If that budget (see Figure 2-3) is to have meaning as a guide to the total project, it must be constantly updated every step of the way in project progress. Upward variations in costs should be called to management's attention prior to final commitment in order to avoid unpleasant surprises.

SPACE REDECORATION

Redecorating, on the other hand, requires no study to prove that the space works; it is in fact the acceptance of the existing layout, but not the appearance of the space. Complete redecoration would mean a totally new approach to design, without touching the layout. This could mean all new furniture, furnishing accessories, draperies, ceilings, lighting, floor coverings, wall coverings, finishes, colors, cabinet work, art program, graphics, and anything else that would change the "look" of the space. Or it could mean only part of that effort—the redesign and refurnishing of a room or an area or a department or, perhaps, just a repainting of the entire premises.

How much or how little should be done depends on the motivating factor for redecorating and the ability of the company to finance it. The first step should be to update the budget estimate for such redecoration. (See Figure 3-2.) If the total job costs more money than the company wishes to invest, it should be determined how the money available can be spent to achieve the maximum results. In some instances best results would be achieved in those areas frequented by the company's clients: areas such as the reception room, salesrooms, conference rooms, or the executive area. In other instances a change in general environment would be beneficial to staff morale and productivity. Each company has to make its own decision as to which direction, other than total redecoration, to take. The decision is easier to make if a detailed budget estimate of a total job is available for study. Once that decision is made, the final steps of planning, design, and working drawing preparation can get under way.

Section III: Project Staffing

The aspects of *real estate* that may be part of the relocation problem are numerous enough to require the help of people with specialized knowledge. Although all these people could conceivably be found under the roof of one real estate company, they are described here as separate talents. The fees of all, except the real estate broker, should be either a flat sum agreed upon in advance or based on time spent on the job, payable according to an agreed-upon schedule of hourly rates for each person or category of effort involved.

REAL ESTATE CONSULTANT

The real estate effort should start with an analysis of existing real estate commitments. This should include all property presently owned and/or rented, the involvements in each, the impact of those involvements on relocation, and recommendations as to what can and should be done about these commitments. The recommendation and the plan of action to be taken could entail the preparation of marketing plans for the conversion of the property or for its disposal by sale, lease, or sublease. Should a real estate broker be required for such sale or lease, the real estate consultant would guide and coordinate that effort.

In a relocation, the consultant should work closely with the specialist in location studies, helping to assess property values, neighborhoods, rental schedules, zoning laws, and locality tax problems. If property is to be acquired, the consultant will prepare an investment analysis and negotiate for the property.

If space is to be rented, the real estate consultant should play a very important role in the preparation of the comparative analysis made of the buildings under consideration. His or her ability to negotiate favorably for a client is of major importance. The areas of negotiation will include the rent, the lease, and the work letter portion of the lease. Sometimes a dollar allowance can be negotiated in lieu of work and sometimes in addition to work. Sometimes the cost of work can be amortized over the length of the lease as a rent inclusion. Needless to say, there is no end to the ways in which a lease can be negotiated and an experienced consultant is more than worth the fee.

REAL ESTATE BROKER

The real estate broker is usually part of a rental situation. If he or she is given exclusive representation, this can include the analysis of several buildings in a specific locality. However, the broker's expertise rarely goes deeper than that. He or she too can provide negotiating know-how, but since the broker's fee is based on a percentage of the total rent to be paid (the published fee scale is usually set by the local real estate board), there is the danger of a conflict of interest. The broker who is chosen to represent the company should be well known by the company or come highly recommended by others who have used his or her services.

LOCATION CONSULTANT

The location consultant should help to establish critical corporate objectives. Within the framework of these objectives he or she should recommend various locations and prepare a series of comparative evaluations which cover the local conditions and sites in extensive detail. These evaluations should include studies of the future of the area, demographic analysis, labor market studies, housing availability, area cost analyses for building and maintenance, availability of required outside business services, and communication and transportation studies. This consultant service can also include site negotiations, site engineering studies, negotiations for access road commitments, and utility extensions.

PERSONNEL RELOCATION CONSULTANT

This service includes the development of a corporate policy for handling personnel problems in a corporate relocation. The analysis leading to such a policy should cover the projected costs of severance pay for those people not moving as well as all the costs involved for those relocating. A complete employee survey should be prepared and a

program initiated for orientation, counseling, and home-finding assistance that would
be monitored closely until all personnel have been properly accounted for.

Possible sources for real estate talent include:

- Local real estate board
- Recommendations from companies that have had relocation experience

CONSTRUCTION MANAGER

Before describing the next talent, definitions will help clarify possible confusions. The construction manager is a relatively new comer to the construction scene, and no two people seem to interpret this role in quite the same way. The following definitions describe the roles of the construction manager and the general contractor as they are interpreted in this book:

General contractor. The company charged with the actual construction of the building, either through competitive or negotiated bid. All of the general contractor's work will be done under management instructions to bidders or under instructions from the construction manager. The general contractor fee is generally a percentage of the cost of the work. (For a more complete description of the role of the general contractor, see "Section IV: Project Staffing.")

Construction manager. An independent consultant, experienced in construction, who will oversee all phases of construction from planning and excavation through occupancy, control expenditures, expedite deliveries, supervise construction and installation, and audit the dollars spent. The construction manager's fee is unrelated to costs.

The role of the construction manager is a many-faceted one. It may be filled by the project director, by an in-house talent, by a general contractor, or by someone else hired specifically for the job. In any event, the person who fills this role must be someone with a great deal of knowledge and wide experience in construction. (How the general contractor may also act as the construction manager will be discussed in the last section of the book. If the two roles are handled by one person, it is wise to have someone else do the construction auditing.)

The construction manager's first major contribution to the project, having already supplied some of the cost information in the feasibility stages, will be to aid in the preparation of the work letter. He should be able to be specific about many of the materials to be listed in the work letter and to help with the descriptive phraseology that otherwise could lead to more than one interpretation after the work has been completed and audited. For example, "tempered glass entrance doors," specified in a work letter, were thought to mean Herculite doors by the designer, but not by the landlord. Someone more knowledgeable in construction could have written the work letter to avoid the argument over dollars that took place after the client had moved into the space.

Next, the construction manager can be of inestimable help to the designer in the selection of materials and by giving advice on construction details and installation methods. Intelligently approached, this can help reduce total costs by a considerable amount without endangering or encroaching upon the desired end results of design. This is a sensitive area and one in which the construction manager's building expertise must be matched by an understanding of the program approved by the client. Aesthetic, emotional, and operational considerations have gone into the planning of this business home and all within the financial framework that should be helped, not hindered, by the construction manager. This is another problem that can be adroitly handled by a capable project manager.

The construction manager will help in the bidding process and be directly involved in all details if the bid is to be a negotiated one. He will, of course, be a major factor throughout the construction phase of the work, creating and administering the schedules for delivery and installation of materials, checking on the adherence to plans and specifications, minimizing the effect of change orders on costs and schedules, and generally supervising and auditing all details of construction, from the beginning of the job through to the completion of installation.

The construction manager should be compensated by a monthly retainer or by a salary for the duration of the job or any other mutually satisfactory arrangement for the payment of a predetermined fee.

Possible sources for construction manager talent include:

- American Institute of Architects
  1735 New York Avenue N.W.
  Washington, D.C. 20006

- *Buildings*
  427 Sixth Avenue S.E.
  Cedar Rapids, Iowa 52406

- Building Owners and Managers Association
  1221 Massachusetts Avenue N.W.
  Washington, D.C. 20005

LEGAL ADVISOR

The need for legal help in the relocation process is tied almost exclusively to real estate matters. It is necessary, therefore, to make certain that advice comes from an attorney well versed in all phases of real estate law. He or she must be capable of handling all the legal details of leases and work letters and of subleasing space for which the company already has a commitment. When required to do so, the legal advisor should be able to guide rezoning applications through the local government agencies and to help in any other governmental involvement that the relocation may occasion. Of lesser importance will be the legal aid needed for approving or drawing up contracts between the company and whatever other specialists may be retained during the course of the project.

The legal fees usually cover the attorney's time and that of any assistants plus out-of-pocket expenses for phone calls, transcripts, court expenses, etc. Some companies have in-house legal staffs whereas others have attorneys under retainer, but in either case, the specialized help required for real estate law makes it necessary to augment the help normally available.

ARCHITECT

The architect who will design the building should do so within the framework of the program set up by the space planner. With all effort coordinated by the project manager, the preliminary, experimental steps of building design must meet all the space needs programmed for company use. Each suggested size and shape of building, size and shape of floors, and the building core configuration should be carefully tested against the layout needs of typical company departments. The same kind of tests should be applied to each possible building design in order to analyze the efficacy and the costs for structural systems and mechanical systems. These systems should be worked on by both structural and mechanical engineers. Sometimes this engineering help is available through the architectural office (with the engineering fees included in the architectural fee). At other times, the engineering effort is hired separately, but it still should be done in conjunction with and under the direction of the architect. The architect should also be responsible for coordinating site analysis work and preparing all the working drawings and should work closely with the construction manager during the working drawing preparation and during the bid negotiations. He or she should be expected to do a final audit and to certify the building as meeting all design requirements, and should prepare and sign any documents needed for the procurement of required certificates of occupancy.

The amount of design and specification effort required of the architect for interior elements of the building should be decided upon with the project manager, the space planner, and the interior designer. In a multiple-occupancy building the architect is often charged with specifying all interior design elements such as ceilings, lighting fixtures, doors, hardware, and partitions. In a single-occupancy building, all this is usually the responsibility of the interior designer and space planner, whose specifications should more closely reflect the end use of these elements in furthering the company image and space efficiency.

Possible sources for architectural talent include:

- American Institute of Architects
  1735 New York Avenue N.W.
  Washington, D.C. 20006

- *Architectural Record*
  1221 Avenue of the Americas
  New York, New York 10020

- *Progressive Architecture*
  600 Summer Street
  Stamford, Connecticut 06904

ENGINEERING

Engineering consists of both structural and mechanical engineering. The structural engineer is responsible for the structural system of the building (steel, poured concrete, etc.) and will make any changes or additions necessary for tenant occupancy, including extra floor-load capacities, stairways, shafts for material handling, and anything else of a structural nature. The mechanical engineer will plan the heating, ventilating, and air conditioning systems and all other utility requirements such as electrical and plumbing. He or she will prepare all the engineering drawings for work required by the tenant plans, making sure that everything done for the tenant is accomplished within the capabilities of the building system.

For a multiple-occupancy building, the engineering fees consist of two parts: one covering the basic building work (usually a percentage of the cost for constructing and/or installing the engineering elements specified) and the other consisting of a flat fee of x cents per square foot to cover the engineering plans to be done for the tenant work. For a single-occupancy building, the engineering fees are usually a percentage of costs of all specified items for both the basic building and the occupants' space.

Possible sources for structural and mechanical engineering talent include:

- American Society of Civil Engineers
  345 East 47th Street
  New York, New York 10017

- Recommendation from the architect

- *Engineering News Record*
  1221 Avenue of the Americas
  New York, New York 10020

IV
Developing
the Plan

11 Design

The design stage is one of the most exciting of the project, if for no other reason than that it is the most visible. The excitement and the visual reward come first from setting the design criteria, and then from watching and participating in the development of the design, as it evolves from the two dimensions of drawings to the three dimensions of reality.

EXTERIOR AND INTERIOR

If there is to be a new building, the design effort is concerned with the shell of the building, or its *exterior design,* and with the elements within that shell, or the *interior design.* Because the building is erected to house a business operation and help it work as a well-integrated business machine, it must, like any successfully designed product, be planned from the inside out. The parts of this "machine" must be so planned as to mesh and interact properly before the housing can be designed.

The space planner, whether separate from or part of the architectural firm, has determined the company's space needs and the way in which that space must be planned. Those requirements provide the basic program from which the architect works when planning the building shell and the size, shape, and core configuration of the floors.

The architect should be present at the *design meeting* and should suggest any additional items to be included for discussion. He or she should then be prepared to include for design consideration, in addition to the space program already prepared by the space planner, any new decisions made at the design meeting that concern interior space use and that may have impact on the overall building plan. These plans are really a refinement of earlier, preliminary plans done when management first approved the project.

The work of the architect, engineers, space planner, and interior designer will be coordinated by the project manager, who will see to it that all elements of the program are included in the plans. It will be the project manager who, as early as possible in the design phase, will assign the responsibilities for choosing and creating the various elements of building design. He or she will decide whether the architect or the interior designer will be responsible for the lighting, the selection of partitions, doors, hardware, floor covering, wall finishes, elevator cabs, etc. These are not very easy decisions to make, but no matter what the answer, the coordinating responsibility (and so the end result) rests with the project manager.

A problem that arose on a project will illustrate the importance of this coordinating role. A building was to be erected for the single occupancy of a company. The space planner was retained first to determine the number of square feet to be provided and the best size, shape, and number of floors to house the company most efficiently. After this program had been completed, the architects were chosen to design the building. When it came to designing the interior elements, a major confrontation arose between architect and interior designer/planner. Each thought he should be responsible for the walls, doors, floors, hardware, ceiling system and lighting: the architect, because he wanted to tie all these elements into the building shell design, and the interior planner, because he thought it should all be part of interior environment and the company use of space. Both were equally persuasive in their arguments. Unfortunately, an inexperienced management was unable to adjudicate the problem in the best interests of the project. They compromised by having the architect design the ceiling and the lighting while the planner did the rest. The result was that there was no compatibility among the elements. Although there was a high level of lighting intensity, it was inappropriately placed and inadequate for the space it was supposed to illuminate. An experienced project director would have understood the problem immediately and either assigned responsibilities differently or coordinated the design efforts of architect and planner to assure compatible results.

The principal factor in making a decision should be the desired end use which, in most cases, will indicate that the specifier of those elements used in the interior of the building should be the interior designer. It is the designer's job to set the environmental theme for the company, and all interior design features should be in harmony with that theme. To be more specific about it, if the interior designer has planned or selected the work stations, it hardly seems logical for anyone else to select and locate the lighting source required to illuminate that station.

The architect's design presentation, which should take place as soon after the design meeting as possible, will be similar to the interior design presentation although, logically, not nearly so detailed. A budget estimate of costs, submitted with the design presentation, should be prepared with the help of the engineers and the construction manager.

Interior design plays a role in every kind of project whether it be relocation to a new, single-occupancy building that some companies will need or the simple redecoration of some or all of the areas that make up the company home in the space it presently occupies.

The purpose of this chapter is not to make architects or designers of its readers. It is intended, as is the book itself, to help provide a broader understanding of the total scope of a relocation project. Armed with this knowledge, company personnel can help their retained consultants to understand the company better and thus be better able to interpret its operational requirements and design needs.

DESIGN MEETING

The success of design depends upon how well it reflects the desired company image, how well the company people can live within it, and how well it stays within the framework of the dollars allotted to it. To meet these requirements for success, two things must be done promptly and thoroughly. The first, which hopefully at this point in project development will be well under way, is to get and to keep the budget updated and monitored on almost a day-to-day basis. The second is to prepare for and hold the *design meeting*, which is really the second of the orientation meetings discussed previously. The key words are "prepare for"! Top management must be at this meeting and will be asked to provide the guidelines and decisions that will help set the character of design and of the project itself. In order to do so intelligently, those people who are the decision makers must be given, in whatever form is appropriate, all the facts that have been gathered through the questions, studies, and analyses that have been going on since the project first started.

The first documents that should be shown are those drawings which will summarize, for top management, the progress of planning to date. They should be on display so that they can be referred to easily during the meeting to stimulate design discussion. The drawings should include the preliminary plans and preliminary renderings of the building (if there is to be a building), profiles showing departmental relationships from floor to floor, and the space studies as they have been "finalized" to date. The assumption is that none of these drawings will be entirely new to management and that, since management has already approved them, almost no time at all will have to be taken from this meeting for further decision discussions concerning them. There are certainly enough things to be talked about at the design meeting to preclude getting bogged down in talk about items that should have been decided upon previously.

If there are some legitimate reasons for questions or suggestions concerning these "finalized" preliminary drawings, it would be best, unless the problem is a major one that could bring about equally major conceptual changes, to hold these questions until after the design meeting. There may be quite a number of people in attendance, only a few of whom should be or need be involved in space study or building discussion. It should also be kept in mind that in any project of this nature nothing is really finalized until the building is built, the space constructed, the furniture and equipment delivered and installed, and the company moved in and operating. Even then changes may take place! During every step of the way (the preparation of design and working drawings, bidding, equipment selection, purchase authorization, construction, and installation) new ideas may have a bearing on and change original concepts. A design idea for a circular conference room when the space study shows a rectangular one will certainly force changes in space use and therefore change the original space study. What is termed "finalized" for the design meeting is but a springboard for design—a framework of space relationships that should be maintained subject only to design editing.

The people who must be in attendance at the design meeting representing the company are those in top management; the chairman of the board, the president, and anyone else whose input on the company image as represented by design and environment is important to the end product. In addition, the company will be represented by the project manager and the project director. The outside consultants in attendance should include the architect (if there is one), the space planner, the interior designer, and any required members of their staffs.

The project manager should bring management up to date on the status of the job, using whatever documents are available to help do so. He or she should review all the decisions made to date, reminding management, for example, of what led to the decision to locate and build in the suburbs of a city other than the one in which they are now located. This review should also include the facts that there will be a new system for handling paper, dictating, producing, filing, and mailing and a new way of handling supplies. It should be explained that there will be two new departments and corporate rather than departmental conference rooms, and that all these are to be housed in a series of buildings in a campus arrangement. The project manager should then review the projections of company growth that have led to the size of the facilities to be built, the concept of space use agreed upon, the size, shape, and design features of the building, and the plans of the floors within the buildings, including the departmental space studies done on those plans. To provide management with as complete a review as possible, the project manager should have the retained consultants explain those parts of the project for which they have been and are responsible.

After the review, the design meeting should be chaired by the interior designer since most of the questions and most of the discussions will concern the work he or she will be doing in design, lighting, flooring, partitions, wall covering, furniture, and all the other things that are an integral part of the office environment.

The interior designer must attempt to stimulate management people to verbalize about all the areas of design interest, starting with, and spending most of the discussion time on, the general subject of company "image." In some cases, it would be a good idea to ask the interior designer to prepare a checklist of questions which could be distributed, in advance of the meeting, to give those attending an opportunity to prepare for the questions. Such a checklist should be edited to fit each specific situation and tailored to intelligently reflect operational decisions already made. The following is a typical questionnaire, prepared to be distributed prior to the meeting:

DESIGN QUESTIONNAIRE

The purpose of the Design Meeting, to be held on _____, is to help the designer of our new space to learn as much as possible about our company—its history, the public it serves, the people that work for it, and the "image" it would like to project to our people and to the public. What we say will do much to guide the designer in preparing the design approach for our new home and in preparing the budget estimate of costs to accomplish that approach.

Please read the questions that follow and be prepared to talk at length on the subjects they cover or on any other subjects that you think will aid the consultants in designing our space:

- What is the history of our company: its age, its position in the industry, and anything else that makes it unique in the industry or in the business community as a whole?

- In how many places is the company located? Where? Is there a unifying theme of design presently in use? Are there design standards that should be continued—a logo, colors, furniture standards?

- Is there a particular design look that you think it should have for its visitors or its staff?

- Do you think design should reflect progress, stability, richness, dignity?

- What period or style do you think will best reflect the look you want—contemporary or traditional?

- Who are the company visitors—customers, suppliers, other company people?

- Is there any material, products, literature, ads, or other things that should be featured in displays or wall decorations in sales or conference or reception rooms?

- Are there personal or corporate color likes or dislikes?

- Please give consideration to an art program—original paintings and/or drawings, sculpture, reproductions, graphics, with or without a unifying theme reflecting the company, the industry, the locality, or anything else you can think of.

- Although basic information has already been gathered concerning the things that will be required in the board room, conference rooms, sales rooms, and library, please voice any further thoughts you may have about their appearance or utility. Private offices will be discussed individually with each executive whose office is to be considered as a special design area, and a day and time will be set for such discussions. Unless management has other ideas, all other private offices will be planned with standard furniture and furnishings, with each occupant given a choice of chairs, fabric colors, carpet colors, and drapery colors, all from a controlled range of choices.

Since this questionnaire would be edited for each situation, it could conceivably be a much more voluminous document. It could include discussions about all the facilities management had already decided would be part of the new home, such as lunchrooms, recreation areas, reception rooms, auditoriums, and any other specific areas. An experienced designer would enlarge the discussions and get from the company people such information as would be the most help. From this he or she should be able to create an exciting design approach for the total company space.

BUDGET

But the first thing that the designer should prepare, after the design meeting, is an updated *budget* of the money that will have to be spent to meet the client's design desires. To begin anything approaching a design presentation would be foolish indeed unless and until management has approved the costs.

The project is also at the point where the design budget must not only be updated but spelled out in more detail than it has been up to now. A workable budget estimate form should detail, on a room-by-room and area-by-area basis, the costs for lighting, doors, partitions, ceilings, electrical work, telephone conduits, plumbing, furniture, furnishings, and anything else of a design nature such as cabinet work and the art program. If there is a lease and a work letter, the budget should cover all items in excess of the allowance defined in that work letter.

A more detailed budget is prepared at this point because the choices of design and construction elements have been narrowed down and are now less generalized. It is no longer desirable to deal with lump sum amounts. In fact, it now becomes possible to trade off dollars in order to help make design more meaningful. For example, it may be wise to spend more money on a reception or sales area in order to increase the impact of that area as a "selling tool," and to compensate by spending less on an area where the saving will have little effect on the end product.

Management's problem at this point, and it is a difficult one, is to understand that the dollars represented in this preliminary budget presentation are, in many cases, only estimated expenditures. The budget may show an estimated cost of $10,000 for the furniture in the president's office, but there are no pictures of desks, or chairs, or samples of fabric to show what the $10,000 represents in actual furniture or furnishings. The difficult thing to grasp is that the budget presentation is not the session at which decisions are made about aesthetics. It is the time when the experienced designer presents an approximation of what the costs will be for those things the client has requested. Approval of the budget is a signal to the designer that the anticipated overall dollar expenditure is approved, and that specific plans may proceed from there within the framework of allotted dollars. The final decision will come when dollars and aesthetics are placed side by side at the design presentation. This is when management begins to approve the specifics of what is being purchased for each dollar that will be spent.

An example of a budget form that should be prepared by the designer, with help as needed from the space planner, architect, and construction manager, is shown in Figures 11-1 and 11-2. These budget worksheets and the budget summary are designed to show three sets of figures: *preliminary* figures submitted after the design meeting, the figures as *edited* after the first submission, and the *design* presentation figures. These last figures, in total if not in detail, should equal or be very close to the total allocated in the edited budget.

Management's staff will have helped in the preparation of the edited budget, participating with the designer in a study of the preliminary figures to determine how the dollars should be allocated. Once the edited budget has been approved, design gets under way in earnest.

Management's acceptance of the design (the style, the understanding of the individual, the understanding of the corporation, the furniture, colors, fabrics, lighting, partitions, and all the other visible aspects of the aesthetic approach to the design of these particular offices) will reflect the designer's ability to interpret management's design aims. The design itself is not relevant to this book. However, since management people will be asked about aspects of design such as lighting and furniture and carpet, they should know enough about these things to discuss them intelligently with the project manager and the designer and thus help make decisions.

Partitions can be "dry wall" (sheetrock of varying thicknesses fastened to metal studs), steel, steel and glass, wood, wood and glass, or all glass. They can be of any height desired by the designer, and each has its own sound-attenuating capabilities. Some of these partitions have built-in raceways to carry telephone and electric wire, while others can be designed with raceways if they are desired. All partitions, except glass ones, including those designed especially for open planning, can be designed to accept acoustical material, pin-up displays, or magnetically fastened displays.

Lighting, a prime element in the design of office space, has been studied very closely in the past few years and, partly because of the energy crisis, has undergone some

Figure 11-1   BUDGET FORM WORKSHEET

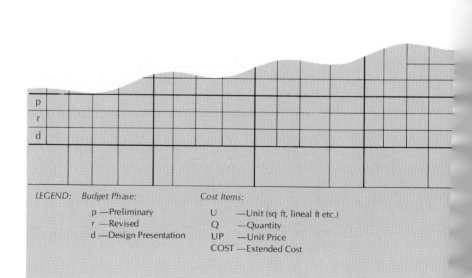

HEATING, VENTILATING AND AIR CONDITIONING/PLUMBING

Phase	LABORATORIES				SPEC. TOILETS				ENG. FEES				PERIPH. UNITS			
	U	Q	UP	Cost	U	Q	UP	Cost	U	Q	UP	Cost	U	Q	UP	Cost
p																
r																
d																
p																
r																
d																
p																
r																
d																
p																
r																
d																
p																
r																
d																

This is one page of the budget. There should be budget coverage for *HVAC/plumbing; electrical work; walls a wall coverings; doors; flooring and ceilings; woodwork and metal fabrication;* and *furniture, furnishings, a accessories.* (Some of these can be combined if there are not many special items under each heading.) Ea

p																
r																
d																

LEGEND: *Budget Phase:*   *Cost Items:*

        p —Preliminary   U   —Unit (sq ft, lineal ft etc.)

        r —Revised   Q   —Quantity

        d —Design Presentation   UP —Unit Price

                           COST —Extended Cost

SPEC. EXHAUSTS								AREA	Phase	TOTALS	H V A C
U	Q	UP	Cost	U	Q	UP	Cost	open areas			
									p		
									r		
									d		
									p		
									r		
									d		
									p		
									r		
									d		
									p		

…de'' should use as many sheets as would be required to describe the costs on an area by area and/or a …om-by-room basis.

									Phase		
									r		
									d		
									p		
									r		
									d		
									p		
									r		
									d		
									p		
							Totals this page		r		
									d		

Figure 11-2 BUDGET FORM SUMMARY SHEET

BUDGET SUMMARY

Phase	HVAC/ plumbing	Electrical work	Walls and covering	Doors	Ceilings
p					
r					
d					
p					
r					
d					
p					
r					
d					
p					
r					
d					
p					

This is a summary of all of the worksheets (see Fig. 11-1), and on it is shown the analysis of job costs, totaled on a trade-by-trade basis. To make the budget easier to understand, the summary should, if possible, be confined to

p					
r					
d					
p					
r					
d					
p					
r					
d					
Totals					
p					
r					
d					

LEGEND: p —Preliminary
            r —Revised
            d —Design Presentation

Woodwork and metal fabrication	Furniture, furnishings, and accessories	Areas	Phase	Total for area
			p	
			r	
			d	
			p	
			r	
			d	
			p	
			r	
			d	
			p	
			r	

one page. If it becomes too complicated to put on one sheet, the "Areas" can be floor-by-floor or any other subdivisions of the total space that can conveniently be placed on a single summary sheet.

			Phase	
			r	
			d	
			p	
			r	
			d	
			p	
			r	
			d	
			p	
			r	
			d	
		Total space	p	
			r	
			d	

radical changes. There was a time when the Illuminating Engineering Society set very rigid standards for the number of footcandles of illumination that should be maintained at desk level. They had a performance chart showing levels of illumination for all categories of office and laboratory and drafting room tasks. Drafting room illumination was set at 200 to 250 fc, auditing and bookkeeping tasks required 150 to 200 fc, and general office work needed 100 to 150 fc. All these figures were calculated on the basis of maintained footcandles of illumination at desk level. ("Maintained" means the output of a lighting fixture six months after its installation, when dust on the tubes and grime on the lens and age in general has lessened the efficiency of the fixture.) For quite a number of years this kind of measurement, varying only in an increase in footcandle requirements over the years, was considered the only way to calculate lighting efficiency. Then, a number of creative lighting experts began to question this concept. The answers they came up with, extremely helpful as they were in providing better light, gained more meaning and a larger audience because the energy crisis forced people to reexamine the way in which energy was being used and wasted. Measuring lighting efficiency by its intensity throughout a room at desk level really meant, according to the lighting experts, throwing a huge amount of light into areas where it was not needed. The lighting consultant advocated, instead, superior light coupled with a marked reduction in energy output.

Lighting consultants can play an extremely important role in space design, and serious consideration should be given to making one a part of the project effort. The potential contribution of lighting consultants is in direct proportion to the size of the project, but they should not be ruled out of smaller jobs where design and designed lighting can be of vital importance.

Carpeting is another area of design about which there is a great deal of confusion. The purchase of carpet represents one of the largest single expenditures in most design budgets. As such it must be specified wisely. The problem stems from having to choose from among thousands of carpet products manufactured by hundreds of mills using a confusing profusion of available fibers. It stands to reason that in such a competitive field, the individual mill representative is not going to have a very objective viewpoint. But the average designer needs help to determine the exact kind of carpet and backing that should be used, the subflooring and underflooring that should be used, the best kind of carpet for access to duct systems, how to make certain that the mill is delivering according to specifications, and a number of other things that, done wrong, can mean dissatisfaction with the installed product. Here again, using a consultant can be a fine insurance policy, helping to protect a sizable expenditure of money. If a knowledgeable, reliable installer is well known by the company or the interior designer, his or her contract could include payment for advice in the selection and specification of the carpet and for approval of the quality of the delivered product. Although carpet is much more expensive than vinyl, vinyl-asbestos, or asphalt tile, the cost of caring for each material could make carpet far less expensive over its usable lifetime.

Sound absorption in most offices can be accomplished effectively with ceiling tiles, carpeting, and drapes. However, problems of *acoustics* in areas such as conference rooms or equipment rooms should be very carefully analyzed. If a sound problem in any one of these areas will be critical, an acoustical consultant should be brought in to help during the planning stage so that his or her specifications and recommendations will be coordinated with design and technical effort. Sound problems are more difficult to solve and cost much more money to cure if they are attacked after the space has been built.

Both the open plan and office landscaping present acoustical problems because of the number of people working in one open area. Many of the partition systems designed for these open plans are covered with sound-absorbing materials, but while helpful to an extent, they do not solve all the sound problems inherent to the open plan. It is wise to seek the advice of an acoustical consultant during the planning stage and for exactly the reasons indicated above.

Furniture that is selected by the designer and approved by the company for its appearance should be put through rather rigid testing before final acceptance. Desks, files, open-plan work stations, and any other pieces of furniture and equipment that will be purchased in large quantity should be tested and compared to similar, competitive lines. If feasible, a prototype test area should be set up, modeled as closely as possible to the plan of the new space and using as many of the elements of design furniture and furnishings as possible. This should include lighting, flooring, colors, and materials so that the testing can be complete, with judgements made on maintenance, workability, and livability. If it is possible to have a test period, it should run from 3 to 6 months. Attention should be paid, over the test period, to such things as the functioning of drawer mechanisms, locks, glides, casters, flooring, lighting, accoustics, the surface appearance of desks and files, fabrics, and all other elements to be tested and judged during this period. Chairs should be sat in by the potential users, and the chairs to be so tested should include secretarial chairs, conference room chairs, executive swivel chairs, visitor chairs, and in fact, all seating that will be used by company personnel and visitors to the offices.

The prototype installation should serve not only as a furniture and equipment test area but, if possible and if relevant, as a design model within which ceiling treatments, partitions and wall treatments, wood finishes, and colors can all be "tried on for size." Prototype areas have been used to test management's reactions to plan concepts and all other design elements that will have an effect on the individual and his or her work in the office. It must be remembered, however, that the model is not installed to get the company's personnel to "vote" on the quality of design. The worst thing that could happen would be to allow this kind of design by committee. Top management and its selected advisors went through an exhaustive search before they retained an interior design firm. Having done so, it would be ridiculous not to abide by their recommendations, unless they are so far off the mark that they have completely misinterpreted everything the company is trying to accomplish in the environment it is trying to create.

That not only would be most unlikely but certainly would have been recognized before a prototype testing area had been set up.

Sometimes, too, the model area will provide an extra dividend. A new concept for the use of glass as a dividing wall was recently tested in a prototype model. While the installation was being made, a new method for handling the glass installation was discovered, which was better and less costly than the method that had been planned. Quite often money-saving shortcuts and design refinements can be accomplished because the model provides an opportunity for an advance look at what would otherwise be an untested finished product.

This discussion of the prototype area is a little out of true chronological order. It could not really be constructed until after the design concept had been presented and approved. It is, however, another reminder to management that nothing is really regarded as having been finally approved, nor should authorization for purchase be issued, until everything to be bought or built has undergone the closest scrutiny possible.

DESIGN PRESENTATION

Preparation of the *design presentation* is the responsibility of the interior designer. The purpose of the presentation is to show management what the designer believes the offices, reception rooms, conference rooms, etc., should be like. The designer will expect to get management's approval of this concept. Then, subject to whatever further inspections and testing management and the designer want to make, management should be prepared to approve the expenditure of the money necessary to implement the concept.

Because so many decisions hinge upon the ability to understand what is being presented, management has the right to want, and the designer has the obligation to provide, the clearest possible kind of presentation. To make it so, the presentation should include some or all of the following clarifying material:

1. *Presentation plans* are the final revised and approved space-study plans of the total space. They should show all the elements of design that can be illustrated on such plans, specifically keying them to renderings, drawings, and models. In addition, these presentation plans should include more detailed, larger-scale plans of any specific areas, such as private offices or a reception room, that may need these details to further clarify the design.

2. *Scale models* of a building can be simple indications of structural masses showing no details at all, or they can depict in miniature every window mullion, block of stone, brick, and detail of exterior design. Models of the interior can show full floors or an area of a floor. Each can be a simple illustration of the major elements of the areas shown on the model or detailed to show every desk, every chair, and every file in the space. It is quite usual for models to illustrate the architectural approach to the building and in many cases to show the landscaping and the surrounding buildings. Models are not usually made of interior spaces except to illustrate some element of design not easily shown in a drawing. There are a few large companies with more than one building that use complete models of each of their floors in each of their buildings. On the models all partitions, desks, chairs, cabinets, etc., are shown as an aid to the companies' space-planning departments. If they need more space in a particular department, they will test the desired changes on the model before committing the changes to the three dimensions of the actual space.

3. *Renderings* are drawings (usually perspective drawings and sometimes isometric drawings) in color or in black and white. They are prepared to illustrate what a building looks like, or a floor of a building, a room, a part of a room, a piece of furniture, a detail of a cabinet, or anything else that can best be shown and explained through the medium of a drawing.

4. *Photographs* of the pieces of furniture and equipment that are being recommended, as well as samples of fabrics, carpets, wall-covering materials, wood finishes, paint colors, glass, and anything else best described in sample form should be assembled as part of the design presentation.

5. Quite often some of the actual *furniture* will be assembled for management's assessment. This "showing" would take place even if prototype areas were to be built later for testing purposes. It should be shown because usually the furniture gathered in the company offices is the furniture that will be used by the executives. The chairs, swivel and conference room, should be brought in to be judged for both design and comfort before the final decision to purchase them is made. If the furniture is to be shown to the executives on the same day that the design presentation is held, the furniture should be kept in another room and not exhibited until the design presentation has been completed. A furniture display might very well be a major distraction from what is a difficult, attention-demanding task. Design presentations, at the end of which important and expensive decisions must be made, can last for many hours. Management must be prepared to give these presentations undivided attention. There are two important "rules" for the conduct of these meetings— no telephone calls should be taken during them, and all questions and comments should be saved until the presentation has been completed.

6. Information about any existing furniture and equipment to be retained should also be included as part of the presentation. Management should be shown, on the plan, exactly where this furniture will be used so that there are no surprises at move-in. If some of the pieces of furniture are to be reupholstered, if wood is to be refinished, or metal is to be sprayed a new color, then samples of fabric, wood finishes, and all colors should be presented exactly as all other samples have been shown. They too should be keyed to whatever other plans or drawings are necessary to illustrate how and where they will be used.

Figure 11-3 AUTHORIZATION FOR PURCHASE—FURNITURE AND FURNISHINGS

DEPARTMENT:			
Description of item	Manufacturer	Cat. No.	Quantity

Each item should be checked and initialed before the form is signed. Only the initialed items should be considered approved for purchase. The company may wish to do the purchasing through its own department rather than have the designer do the purchasing. This Authorization for Purchase should still be prepared by the

Cost of each item is subject
to local tax and all handling charges.

7. *Graphics* as it relates to identification of rooms or areas through signs, sign systems, super graphics, floor and door numbers, directions and directories should be presented in renderings, photographs, or product samples. Plans should be used to show the location of such "signage."

8. An *art program* can be a major cost item. If one is to be considered, the basic concept and an estimate of approximate costs should be made part of the presentation. If the program is aimed only at visual effect through graphics or reproductions, with or without a unifying theme, the whole program can be left in the hands of the designer. If, on the other hand, it is to be a corporate investment in fine art for cultural or monetary reasons, it is best to retain the help of an accredited expert in the particular field of art to be represented in the program.

DATE:				SHEET No.: OF:
Unit cost	Extension	Approximate delivery date	Authorization initials	Remarks

designer, the items initialed, and the form signed before an order can be placed. The "Approximate delivery date" should later be keyed to the expeditor effort.

YOU ARE HEREBY AUTHORIZED TO
PURCHASE THE ITEMS LISTED
ABOVE FOR OUR ACCOUNT

Authorized Signature   Date

The last part of the presentation, after all questions have been asked and all comments made about the visual aspects of the presentation, is the submission of the budget edited to show all the specifics of design. It should give the actual cost of the desks, chairs, fabrics, carpets, files, drapes, and even the accessories that are part of the presented design concept. The budget should also show the estimated costs of the cabinet work, paneled walls, and other elements not yet detailed and sent out for competitive bids.

The *authorization for purchase,* as shown in Fig. 11-3, is prepared by the designer after mangement has approved the items to be bought. The form may be prepared for submission at the end of the design presentation, or it may not be submitted until everything has been tested in the prototype installation. In any event, such an authoriza-

Figure 11-4   FURNITURE ASSIGNMENT CHART

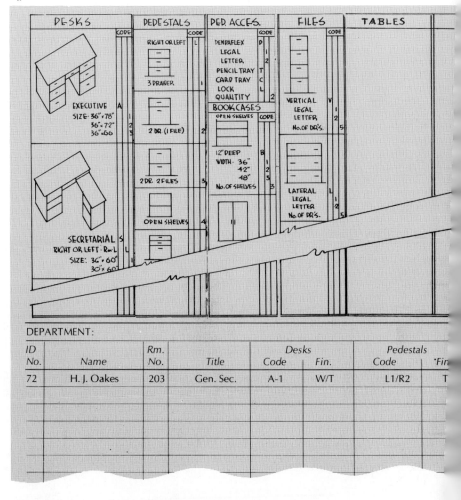

DEPARTMENT:							
ID No.	Name	Rm. No.	Title	Desks		Pedestals	
				Code	Fin.	Code	Fin.
72	H. J. Oakes	203	Gen. Sec.	A-1	W/T	L1/R2	T

This form should include all items of furniture and the accessories to that furniture, that will be purchased in quantity. The drawings and/or the descriptions of these items can be made part of the form (see above) or can be separate from it. Detailed illustrations of this kind will make it easier to check the requirements for each person.

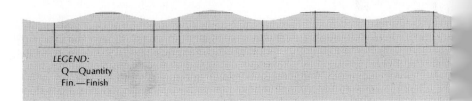

LEGEND:
  Q—Quantity
  Fin.—Finish

WORK STATIONS	FINISHES	CHAIRS	CREDENZAS

FLOOR: DATE:

Pedestal accessories		Files			Tables			Work Stations		
Code	Fin.	Code	Fin.	Q	Code	Fin.	Q	Code	Fin.	Q
P1/T/L	T	V/2/4	T	6						

and work station.

The summary of this Assignment Chart can be prepared on the Authorization for Purchase form (Fig. 11-3).

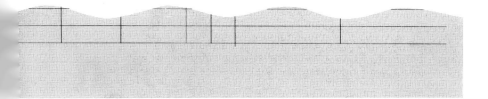

tion form should describe the items including such relevant information as color, finish, manufacturer, catalog number, quantity to be purchased, the unit price, and the total price. The form should also show any additional costs to which the company will be subject such as delivery charges, sales tax, and installation charges. If it is not possible for the designer to supply exact costs for these things, it should be indicated on the form that these charges will later be added to the costs of the actual items to be purchased.

Costs for refinishing and reupholstering any existing furniture should be included on the authorization form. These should include not only the cost of labor for the work to be done but also the cost of fabrics or other material required.

If there are to be large quantities of new desks, files, work stations, and other things with a variety of different components to be ordered for them, a selection and assignment chart should be prepared by the designer. This should be completed and submitted for company checking before or at the same time that the authorization for purchase is submitted. This furniture assignment chart, a sample of which is shown in Figure 11-4, should show exactly what is to be ordered for each employee in each department. It should illustrate the items to be assigned in whatever detail is necessary to make it easy to understand. The tabulated information on this chart can then be consolidated on the authorization form. It can also be used when setting up a permanent inventory of furniture and equipment.

Before discussing the inventory form, there is one furniture problem that all relocating companies face—what to do with the old furniture and equipment. Getting rid of it is not always a simple matter. There was a time when charitable organizations were delighted to get used office furniture and put it to use in their own offices. But during one period in very recent history so many companies moved and purchased new furniture in the process that charitable organizations got more furniture than they could possibly use. Most nonprofit organizations no longer snap up offers of furniture. However, it is still the first direction that should be pursued. In addition to being a good deed, it may also be a tax-deductible one.

Some companies like to give their employees an opportunity to buy any furniture or equipment that they might want for their own use. Desks, chairs, typewriters, and adding machines are some of the things an employee may want. The company could give these things away or charge a nominal amount for them. Anything left could then be offered to a charitable organization or failing to find one willing to take the furniture or equipment, it may be possible to find an organization that has selling outlets. Hospitals, religious organizations, the Salvation Army, and others run thrift shops from which they sell anything given to them. Also, there are furniture dealers, many of whom do a considerable business in the sale or leasing of used furniture. Sometimes it is possible to package the purchase of new furniture with the sale of the old, since many dealers handle both new and used furniture. There have been times when the award of a contract for the purchase of new furniture was made because of the amount of credit given for the used furniture.

Equipment such as typewriters, adding machines, and calculators can be disposed of in the same way as furniture. It can, in fact, be made part of the same deal. But there is also one other direction that can be explored. Many localities have guidance and rehabilitation centers where vocational training for the handicapped often includes the study of business machine repairs. Institutions of this kind are always in need of equipment that can be used by the students. If there is a problem in locating such a facility, contact the state office of vocational rehabilitation (practically every state has one or something like it) and it will help.

Some companies, particularly smaller ones, may want new furniture and equipment for their relocation but hesitate to order these things because of the heavy cash outlay their purchase may mean. A satisfactory solution for such a company could be to lease the furniture and equipment. Leasing is generally more expensive in the long run, but it does have distinct tax advantages in addition to allowing the company to spread the financial burden over a manageable period of time.

There are many different lease arrangements that can be made. Terms can run from 2 to 10 years; arrangements can be made for suppliers to deliver, service, and repair

Figure 11-5   COMPUTERIZED INVENTORY

Item	Type	Size	Cond.	Color	Mater'l.	Top	LOCATION		
							Dept.	Bldg.	Floor/Rm.

A code book or code sheets should be part of this inventory record and should illustrate with pictures and samples, all items, types, sizes, etc.

    ITEM   would be coded to chairs, desks, files, etc.
    TYPE   would be coded to a style, a manufacturer or a source of supply.
    SIZE   would be coded to size of top, number of drawers, lineal feet, etc.
  COND. would be shown as good or poor
  COLOR would be coded to fabric or to finish color
MATER'L would be coded to wood, steel, glass, etc.
    TOP   would be coded to leather, formica, wood, etc.

With all of this information computer stored and updated for changes, additions or relocations, it is a very simple matter to quickly obtain a print out showing where a specific piece of furniture is located, where all desks of a particular style can be found, how many four drawer legal files there are and where they are located, and, in fact, provide any kind of furniture, furnishings and equipment information that may be required at any time.

leased items during the terms of the contract; there can be various termination options including re-lease or buy at a preset amount.

Depending upon the total amount in question, dealers may finance the leasing themselves or arrange for it through a bank or a company specializing in financing lease deals. The contract does not have to be confined to furniture and equipment. It has been known to include carpeting, drapes, pictures, and all other accessories.

The necessity for an inventory of furniture and equipment is in direct proportion to the size of the company and the number of buildings and office spaces it occupies. Properly updated, the inventory can be a very valuable document that will make it much easier to keep track of the location of everything the company owns. It can do this despite the constant changes and shifts of personnel and departments that is almost a day-by-day happening in so many companies. Space can be kept more homogeneous in appearance because similar styles of furniture can be kept together. If the listing is put on a computer, any required piece of furniture or equipment can be quickly located, items that may be in need of repair can be easily identified, stored furniture can be quickly found when needed for new people or a new project, and all furniture and equipment can be programmed under any number of subheads that might prove useful to the company.

The kind of inventory information that can be computer-stored is shown in Figure 11-5. This inventory should include all the new furniture and equipment purchased and, of course, all the old furniture and equipment that is being retained. Simpler forms, as shown in Figures 4-4A and 4-4B, were discussed in connection with the original inventory taken at the start of the project. These forms would provide a good permanent inventory for smaller companies.

12 Working Drawings and Specifications

After the design presentation has been completed and all approvals either have been obtained or are sufficiently close to being obtained so that no major changes are likely, work on the project will proceed to the next step: the preparation of the *construction documents*. These documents consist of working drawings, specifications, and all other rules, regulations, and instructions necessary for bidding and building the project.

The construction manager will play an important role in this effort, checking all working drawings and details of construction and making certain that all materials and products conform to earlier decisions. The construction manager will also approve any new materials, products, and methods of construction and check specifications and bid documents.

In many instances the *architect's working drawings* and the *working drawings for the interior space* will be done by separate professional entities. It will be the project manager who will see to it that these efforts are coordinated either by establishing a working relationship between architect and the planner/designer or by assuming the role of liaison. This requires not only initial coordination, but constant recognition of the fact that any changes in plans, before construction is completed, can have a chain reaction on related, and sometimes seemingly unrelated, elements of planning. For example, in one installation, desks were located by plan and placed directly over an under-floor duct run. This was done to make telephone and electric machine hook-up easier to accomplish. Early in the construction stage, before the floors were poured, the duct location was changed by the engineers, but nobody told the space planner, who had done the furniture plan based on the old location. Since the furniture plan had been the basis for the lighting plan, a change in desk location would have required a major lighting revision. As a result of the lack of coordination, a good deal of costly but avoidable drilling had to be done to tie in the ducts to the desks and to the telephones and the typewriters. Had the change in duct layout been discussed early enough, it might not have been made at all. If it had had to be made, knowledge of that fact passed on to the planner in advance of construction would have meant a simple, relatively inexpensive change in the furniture and lighting plans.

The first thing that the project manager must do to avoid these problems is to initiate a schedule of document distribution that must be rigidly maintained and controlled. It can and should be monitored through a system of letters of transmittal, that would show that all drawings had been sent and received by all the people who were supposed to get them. In addition to the establishment of such a system, responsibility must be assigned to one person to spot and call to the attention of all involved people those areas and kinds of plans that could be affected by any plan revisions.

The architect's working drawings include plans, elevations, sections, and details for construction, electric, plumbing, heating and ventilating, site, utility, and landscape work. The structural, mechanical, and electrical work and the landscape design could conceivably be done by others engaged for those purposes but whose work, in most cases, would be an extension of the architect's work and done under his or her guidance.

The architect's specifications are prose descriptions of all the elements of the working drawings that need further clarification, as well as those that could not be shown in drawing form. These include all requirements for materials and equipment, methods of installation, and standards of workmanship. The specifications will be augmented by any other documents that are needed such as bidding instructions (if the bid is not a negotiated one), including time limitations, methods for submitting bids, and contract forms to be used, as well as permits, licensing, jurisdictional approvals, and reporting and accounting requirements.

The working drawings for interior work also include plans and elevations, sections, and details. The information each contains is very closely related to company operations. Before management signs them as approved, there must be an awareness of what each should contain and what should be checked on each.

PLANS

The earliest drawing that should be prepared after design approval is the *furniture plan*. There are several reasons for giving it top priority. The first reason is to provide assurance that all the furniture and equipment, existing and to be purchased, will fit in the places planned for them despite whatever changes may have been made in plans and concepts since the first space study. Additionally, this plan is actually the point of departure for a lighting plan, telephone and electrical outlet locations, a partition plan, and all design details. The furniture plan will show all furniture and equipment which occupies floor space, such as desks, chairs, tables, files, cabinets, data processing equipment, and work stations. Every item will, of course, be drawn to scale. The plan should be properly coded to indicate which pieces are existing, which are to be purchased for the move-in, and which are for future purchase. A third reason is that the plan can also be used to aid in the preparation of the permanent inventory. It will provide the basic information for the company that will handle the move of existing furniture and for the suppliers who will deliver the new furniture.

Since the position of most telephone and electrical outlets is dependent upon the location of desks, the furniture plan should also be used as the *telephone and electric outlet plan*. On it should be shown and located by dimensions all floor, wall, and ceiling outlets. These outlets are the sources of electricity for typewriters, adding machines, desk lighting, vacuum cleaners, and anything else except ceiling-hung, mounted, or recessed lighting fixtures. On it should be similarly shown and located by dimensions all outlets for telephones. The ceiling outlets shown on the furniture plan are only those related to the ceiling systems that allow power to be brought down from the ceiling for business machines or desk illumination. Power is usually brought down, with these systems, in round or square conduits that become part of the overall design of the area. If any of these light or energy sources is to be switch-controlled, the location of the switch and the plan of wiring from the switch will also be indicated on the furniture plan.

If there is an under-floor duct system, the furniture should be positioned to take maximum advantage of it or the duct layout should be planned to best serve the needs indicated on the furniture plan. Whichever comes first, coordination of the two plans, both initially and for any future revisions, is essential if the problems mentioned before are to be avoided.

There are many other ways to bring electrical power to where it is needed, and there are still more ways being devised constantly. The raised floor, providing space for electric cables between it and the actual floor, has been in use for many years. This system has been used effectively in such places as data processing areas, broadcasting studios, and x-ray and diathermy areas. Another system, presently being tested, uses metallic sheets layered between wood panels. The power, carried by the metal, is tapped by easily installed and easily relocated special "outlets."

The simplest way to bring electrical power to where it is needed is to carry the electric wires in the space between the hung ceiling and the underside of the slab of the floor above. A hole can be punched up through the floor and the wire hooked up to an outlet at that spot. Although not always practical, particularly when the space below is not occupied by the company, this can be the most flexible, least expensive system.

No matter which system is used, the details of it must be indicated on the plan or plans related to its installation and use.

The *construction plan* will show the location, by type and by dimension, of all partitions and doors and, either on it or as a separate document, the schedule of all doors and hardware. It will also carry any elevations, details, and sections of anything of a special nature that is to be constructed and that has to be clarified with dimensioned, detailed drawings. In addition, all plumbing requirements will be shown on this plan along with structural requirements and all information relevant to the HVAC capacity. That includes temperature controls, heat loads from machinery and equipment, as well as any unusual human occupancy anticipated in such areas as meeting rooms or training rooms. Occupancy of this sort must be provided for with additional fresh air, exhausts, and any reheat units needed to warm the room when occupancy is not at its anticipated peak.

The *door and hardware schedules* mentioned before will contain a listing of all doors by size, material, swing (whether right or left hand swing), finish, hinges, lock or latch, and size and type of frame.

The *reflected ceiling plan* will show the type of ceiling or ceilings to be used and will indicate, by type and dimensioned location, all fixtures that hang from, are mounted on, or are recessed in the ceiling. There should also be, either on the plan or as a separate document, a complete schedule of all fixtures and the details pertaining to them. These details should include the manufacturer, catalog number, type of fixture, finish, type and size of bulb required, and any other information necessary for its purchase and its installation. If there are to be drapery pockets, recessed projection screens, ceiling breaks, or any other special items that are ceiling-related, details in sections and cross sections should be drawn on this plan to illustrate the items and show how they should be constructed. The plan should also locate, by type and dimension, the switches required to activate the lights and other energy sources and show a schematic wiring plan to clarify the desired switch control.

Another plan in the set of working drawings is the *paint and flooring or finish plan*. This illustrates the distribution of all floor covering, wall colors and covers such as vinyl, paper, and wood veneers. The plan will be keyed to a schedule of materials and colors, manufacturers and their numbers, and all other details necessary for the purchase and installation of these materials.

Additional drawings that may be required include *elevations, cross sections,* and other *details of design or construction* necessary to augment the plans which make up the set of working drawings.

There is an order of priorities that should be followed in the preparation of these working drawings. The first priority, already discussed, is the furniture plan. After it has been completed, the information necessary for engineering work should be supplied as rapidly as possible. This includes the information for structural changes, heating, ventilating and air conditioning requirements, electrical needs, and plumbing requirements. The engineering drawings can then be completed while the working drawings are being prepared, so that shop drawings (details to help fabrication) can be done by the suppliers involved, materials ordered, and the construction and installation of these elements coordinated with the total project.

The information needed for *structural engineering* includes everything requiring structural changes or additions. This encompasses such things as (1) the delineation of areas where the floor load capacity has to be increased to carry files, books, telephone equipment, or other machinery, (2) the delineation of areas where the floors must be pierced to accommodate staircases, escalators, shafts for dumbwaiters, or other material-handling systems, and (3) areas where it is necessary to create ceiling heights in excess of the standard of the building.

For the *heating, ventilating, and air conditioning (HVAC) engineering,* it is necessary to know anticipated heat loads from lighting, equipment, and people, the required temperature controls for any sensitive or otherwise special areas, the areas in which after-hours air conditioning has to be supplied, and the requirements for special exhausts in kitchens and laboratories. In addition the HVAC engineering drawings will show the schematic layout of duct work. These should be superimposed on the reflected ceiling plans and the work coordinated with the engineers, architects, and interior designers so as to make certain that the ducts and lighting fixtures do not interfere with each other.

Electrical engineering drawings will show the required conduit sizes, wiring diagrams, and circuitry diagrams superimposed on both the reflected ceiling plan with the outlets and switches shown on the furniture plan. These drawings will include diagrams and details of the hook-ups required for HVAC, data processing equipment, laboratories, refrigerators, and any other items requiring more than the standard plug-in outlets.

Telephone engineering requirements include conduit sizes and wiring runs. These will be worked out between the space planner and the telephone company engineer. The telephone company engineer, by the way, will also supply the information about weight loads for the telephone equipment room.

Plumbing engineering will show schematic pipe runs and details of pipe sizes and hook-ups for sinks, basins, toilets, drinking fountains, and anything else requiring a tie-in to water sources. Placement of these things will be established on the construction plan. If there is space on this plan, the engineering details will be done directly on it, and in whatever detail is needed to clearly illustrate the required information.

Specifications, instructions to bidders, and all other instructional documents covering the work to be done, the manner in which it should be done, and the schedules for its completion can be separate from or made part of the same kind of documents issued by the architect. The decision to do so or not depends upon the necessity for the close coordination of shell construction and interior construction. In most cases they can be completely separate documents with construction efforts coordinated only as far as time schedules are concerned.

SPECIFICATIONS

Specifications for architectural and interior work will include written descriptions of all elements of the job from earthwork, sitework, foundations, and structure, right through to paint on the walls, carpeting on the floors, and the clean-up of the premises after all the trades have finished their work. These descriptions should expand on those shown on the working drawings, adding whatever prose details are necessary to assure the correct installation in the desired quality of workmanship of all specified materials and products.

INVITATION TO BID

If the job is to be opened to competitive bidding, an *invitation to bid* with *instructions to bidders* will be sent to selected contractors with a set of working drawings and specifications. The invitation will outline the scope of the work to be done, the anticipated time for project completion, the time, form, and place for bid submission, the contract form to be signed, the required insurance coverages, the applications and permits for which the contractor will be responsible, and any other rules, regulations and stipulations by which the contractor will be bound.

Competitive bids can be submitted in as formal or as informal a fashion as may be desired or required by government or corporate rules. Some companies ask that bids be submitted on forms that they have prepared and that include space for performance references, credit ratings, insurance coverage documents, etc., and that all be submitted in sealed envelopes to be opened at a specific time, on a specific date, and in front of all bidders. Other companies prefer a less formal approach. They compare bids privately, decide which general contractor will do the work, and then enter into final, detailed discussions of prices, subcontractors, and schedules before the final signing of contracts.

If the job is to be done under a *negotiated bid,* a general contractor, satisfactory to management and the project staff, will have been selected soon after the construction manager was chosen. This person will work closely with the construction manager, the architect, the planner, and the designer to further the progress of the project, and will help to determine the costs, expedite deliveries, and deal with subcontractors. The general contractor will, and this is the reason for the negotiated bid in the first place, begin construction at the earliest possible date. Under the negotiated bid system, construction should start much before the completion of construction documents. It can, in fact, save from one-fourth to one-third of the time normally required from the beginning to the end of a job.

Section IV: Project Staffing

LIGHTING CONSULTANT

The lighting consultant must first identify what has to be illuminated and then determine how to light it. In so doing he or she should be working for and with the interior designer to help create the mood and image the designer has envisioned for the space. That means that the lighting consultant should be brought in at the beginning of the design effort, since such expertise, if it is to be used at all, should be brought into the project as early as possible. Like all other special studies that have impact on space use or appearance, this work must be completely integrated with the overall planning rather than be an unsuccessful appendage to a completed product.

Once again it should be stressed that a consultant should be just that. The lighting consultant must not be affiliated with a lighting fixture manufacturer, but should be completely free to specify any manufacturer's product, or even design a fixture or a system, to solve a particular problem. The consultant should not, in any way, be a participant who will receive remuneration for effort expended from the sale of a product.

The lighting expert should help to determine what fixtures should be used where and with what kinds of bulbs, tubes, lenses, and reflectors. He or she should help to decide what areas should be treated with overall illumination, where and how tasks should be lit, and what variations of light and shadow will best help to achieve the maximum of desired design effect. Lighting consultants have been in the vanguard of the movement to conserve energy through proper lighting. It can be assumed, therefore, that their planning work will be aimed to achieve the best results with the greatest possible savings of energy.

The consultant should prepare detail drawings and oversee the preparation of any other drawings dealing with the lighting he or she is designing and specifying.

The fee for this work can be based on a multiple of payroll costs times the hours spent on the job. It can also be a flat fee or a flat fee as an upset against time charges.

Possible sources for lighting consultant talent includes:

- *Contract*
  1515 Broadway
  New York, New York 10036

- Illuminating Engineering Society
  345 East 47th Street
  New York, New York 10017

- *Interiors*
  1 Astor Plaza
  New York, New York 10036

CARPET CONSULTANT

The carpet consultant, like the lighting consultant, should be retained at the start of design consideration. By far the most important part of this consultant's contribution will be an ability to recommend the proper type of floor covering for each area of the project. The recommendations should be based on the type of subflooring existent, the anticipated traffic patterns of people and equipment, the areas most likely to get the greatest amount of dirt, the type of under-floor duct system to be used, and any prevailing statute or ordinance compliances that must be met.

The carpet consultant will work in close coordination with the designer when making material selections to help achieve the colors and textures required by design considerations, and will provide a budget estimate of costs prepared from carpet specifications. His or her layout of material should be aimed to achieve the best utilization of carpet from the recommended widths, seam placements, and pattern direction.

The carpet consultant should help to prepare bid documents pertaining to flooring, advise in the contract-letting decisions, and supervise the installation. He or she will, or should, oversee the manufacturing to make certain that specifications are being adhered to and that there are no dye problems with regular or special colors and fibers, and also set up a program for future cleaning and maintenance of the carpet.

Fee arrangements could be based on time, a flat fee, or a flat fee as an upset against time.

- Carpet and Rug Institute
  P.O. Box 2048
  Dalton, Georgia 30720

- *Contract*
  1515 Broadway
  New York, New York 10036

- *Interior Design*
  150 East 58th Street
  New York, New York 10022

ACOUSTICAL CONSULTANT

The acoustical consultant's work may have impact on both planning and design. If such services are to be used, the acoustical consultant should be brought in just before space study finalization. He or she might, for example, suggest that the noise from a keypunch room may interfere with a training room next to it, an interference that could be eliminated by a minor layout change that would put keypunch storage between the training room and the keypunch room.

Through room configurations, materials specifications, and special constructions, acoustical engineers can help to reduce or eliminate noise from mechanical equipment rooms. In the same way, they can plan acoustically correct conference rooms, meeting rooms, and auditoriums. This effort can be particularly important in open-plan layouts where noise, not properly masked or deadened, can create intolerable working conditions.

The acoustical consultant's major aim is to solve noise problems within the desired design concept. This means that acoustical engineering is not a matter of materials only. If drapes or carpet or acoustical tile ceilings are not part of the basic design, the acoustical demands must be met in other ways. There are innumerable examples of successful solutions within the framework of design integrity.

Here again, fees are based on time and/or a flat fee.

Possible sources for acoustical consultant talent include:

- Acoustical Society of America
  335 East 45th Street
  New York, New York 10017

- *Architectural Record*
  1221 Avenue of the Americas
  New York, New York 10020

• *Progressive Architecture*
600 Summer Street
Stamford, Connecticut 06904

ART CONSULTANT

The art consultant would not be brought in until agreement had been reached concerning the desirability of an art program. He or she becomes important if the company is going to invest large sums of money on original art works. Whether the program theme calls for the purchase of contemporary art or art from any other specific period, it would certainly be wise to engage an expert who "specializes" in the specific period indicated.

If an art dealer becomes the assisting expert, the fee should be arranged and agreed to in advance. It should be based on time or a fixed amount, and the dealer should be willing, by contract, to waive any participation in profit or commissions on the items purchased.

If the art program is to be design-oriented rather than an "investment portfolio," it is quite likely that the designer will be able to guide the art program.

Possible sources for art consultant talent include:

• Art Dealers Association of America
575 Madison Avenue
New York, New York 10022

• Art museums

GENERAL CONTRACTOR

The general contractor is not really a retained consultant under the terms of any definition already given. He or she is a participant whose pay will come not from a flat fee, or one calculated against the hours spent on the project, but rather from a percentage of the cost of the construction work for which he or she will assume responsibility. Contracting work is described here, however, because the contractor will be handling and be responsible for one of the largest, if not the largest, amount of money to be spent on the project. Because of that fact the company should know what to look for when hiring a general contractor, what such work will entail, and how the contractor should be supervised and audited.

Many of the safeguards for the company should be built into the bid documents. As part of the bid submission, general contractors should be asked to provide proof of such things as bonding, insurance (including worker's compensation), and errors and omissions insurance. In addition, their financial reputation and the quality of the work they produce should be carefully checked with subcontractors who have worked for them and with companies for whom they have worked. When checking with companies for whom a particular contractor has worked, it would be wise to question the performance of the subcontractors who usually work with that individual. All this has a distinct bearing on the end product.

From foundation to certificate of occupancy, the general contractor is responsible for the construction of the building, and will be in charge of whatever trades are part of his or her own company and of the subcontractors who perform the rest of the work.

If retained before the plans are completed, on a ''negotiated bid,'' the general contractor will help the construction manager and the architect and interior planner with advice on material selection and construction methods. He or she will schedule the job with the construction manager and, under the negotiated bid plan, fast-track construction by getting it and the ordering of material under way as early as possible; will submit invoices, for work completed or materials delivered, on his or her own behalf and for the subcontractors, attesting to their accuracy; and will then pass the invoices on for approval and payment, through the established chain of responsibility.

If there is no construction manager, the general contractor, under the negotiated bid, can be asked to fill that role, too. If this arrangement is followed, some additional compensation should be given to him for this work. The extra compensation should be a fixed fee worked out in advance. Under such an arrangement, all auditing of general contractor work should be assigned to someone else.

If the bidding is competitive, the general contractor will have been chosen after all the working drawings have been completed and submitted to all eligible bidders. The responsibilities will remain exactly as they are outlined under the negotiated bid, except that the general contractors will not, ordinarily, be called upon for advice on materials and construction methods.

In many cases, the general contractor effort will be audited by the construction manager, the project manager, or a clerk of the works hired specifically for this purpose. Sometimes the architect or the space planner will take on this task, but under no circumstances should the general contractor be his or her own auditor. Who ends up as construction auditor will really depend upon the size of the project and the size of the staff involved in it.

It really makes no difference who does the work as long as the person knows what to do and can handle the job competently. That means understanding the project and the schedules—overseeing the construction work and seeing to it that materials are delivered on time, that installation is both timely and properly carried out, and that all contractor questions are answered, problems solved, and invoices approved for payment when it is proper to do so.

Possible sources for general contractor talent includes:

• *Buildings*
  427 Sixth Avenue S.E.
  Cedar Rapids, Iowa 52406

- *Engineering News Record*
  1221 Avenue of the Americas
  New York, New York 10020

Other Specialists

There are other specialists who could help the project at this point. They could help to put together costs, specifications, and other background information of importance to the company and to the interior designer. In these cases, help should come not from consultants but from sources of supply for both products and services. They can give required information concerning costs and delivery problems for their product, products, or services. Their fee would come, hopefully, from the purchase of the product or service.

This group includes:

- Furniture suppliers and manufacturers

- Equipment suppliers and manufacturers

- Furnishing suppliers

- Repair services

- Refinishing services

- Reupholstering services

Possible sources for equipment suppliers and manufacturers include:

- *Administrative Management*
  51 Madison Avenue
  New York, New York 10010

- *The Office*
  1200 Summer Street
  Stamford, Connecticut 06904

Sources for all other suppliers, manufacturers and services include:

- *Contract*
  1515 Broadway
  New York, New York 10036

- *Interior Design*
  150 East 58th Street
  New York, New York 10022

V
Implementing
the Plan

13   Construction

There is really very little company personnel will have to do as far as construction is concerned, except watch—and worry. The amount of worry will depend upon the competency of the staff and the competency of the consultants charged with the responsibilities for the project. There are, of course, many things that must be done at the start of and during construction.

For example, this is the time to consider the problems of building maintenance and office cleaning, if the company is moving to a building of its own and has no staff maintenance crew. The work can be handled by a service company retained to do so, or the company can assemble its own maintenance staff headed by a building operations manager who will organize and manage the maintenance crew.

The cleaning services will be supplied in the same way—by a company retained to do the housekeeping chores or by an in-house staff. No matter how the problem is resolved, the person who will handle building operations should be brought in when construction starts. This person must get to know, as early as possible, all about the building (and the facilities it contains) which will eventually have to be maintained and kept operating. To watch it being constructed and to discuss operations with the people who planned it, with the people who are building it, and with the people who are installing the equipment will enable the building operations manager to understand it better and maintain it more efficiently. Maintenance and cleaning tasks are described in Chapter 14.

The start of construction can properly be fixed at the time when the first expenditure of money is authorized for material or for construction equipment. Whether the bid is negotiated or competitive, there is a point where the early purchase and stockpiling of material should be considered. If there is a possibility that prices may increase, the material cost plus any costs for stockpiling or warehousing should be weighed against the anticipated price increase and a judgment made for or against early buying. The items often considered for advance purchase include structural steel, lighting fixtures, floor tiles, ceiling tiles, doors, hardware, partitions, and any other storable items that will be purchased in large quantities. Other costly items that can be advantageously purchased in advance are design items such as carpeting, desks, chairs, files, and general office equipment. In determining costs for early purchasing, not only must warehousing costs be considered, but insurance, security, and handling charges also have to be included. To avoid unnecessary costs, arrangements should be made, in advance with the suppliers, for the assembly and installation of these items when they are finally delivered. All damaged material must be repaired and replaced as it would be on an original delivery.

SUPERVISING, EXPEDITING, AND AUDITING

The major company effort to be accomplished during construction is supervisory in character and should be handled by the project manager and project financial officer. It entails a careful analysis of progress reports, demanding additional activity when and where it is required, keeping a close rein on both expected and extra costs and paying bills as they legitimately come due.

Figure 4-3 (Project Time Schedule) illustrates the kind of form that could be used for the progress reports to be kept by the construction manager and submitted at regular time periods to the project manager. The first such report should be a *delivery schedule for construction material*. How detailed it should be, and how detailed the next two forms should be, would depend upon the construction manager in agreement with the project manager. This form, as well as its counterpart *delivery schedule for furniture and equipment,* should list all items to be delivered. For each item listed, the purchase order number should be shown to make it easier to check back on any details of the order that may be required when *expediting* delivery. The manufacturer or supplier of each item should be listed and so should the promised delivery date. Space should be provided for dates (as necessary) for advance calls or letters to the suppliers or manufacturers to monitor the promised delivery. Progress-to-date and delivery completion should be indicated on the form exactly as they are in Figure 4-3. The same system of marking can be used on the *construction schedule form,* the third progress report to be kept by the construction manager. The form can be used to chart and monitor basic construction items on a total building basis, on a floor-by-floor basis, or on a combination of both.

The construction manager will keep the financial officer advised of progress and will also submit bills that are approved for payment. These include applications for partial payments for work completed or material delivered as well as final payments at the conclusion of the project. To make sure that everything is kept in orderly fashion, arrangements should be made for the regular submission of requisitions. This is usually done once a month.

The interior designer or specifying specialist will help the construction manager keep track of the scheduled delivery of all furniture and equipment. The delivery schedule will be kept up to date by the specifier and submitted, at regular intervals of time, to the construction manager and to the project manager. The project manager will also approve requisitions and invoices for these items for furniture and equipment, passing them on to the financial officer for payment. All such invoices should be checked against the original contracts and purchase orders.

Few jobs get done without some changes or additions being made during the course of construction, installation, and company move. The major problem posed by these changes is to make sure that neither the changes nor the charges for them get out of control. This requires very careful organizing by the project manager with total back-up by top management. Rules of procedure must be clearly set and rigidly adhered to with no infractions allowed. The procedure starts with a request for a change or an addition. Anyone making such a request should do so only through the construction manager, who, in turn, will follow the set procedure for getting a price for the change from the contractor or supplier involved. The project manager will then get approval from top management and/or the financial officer, sign a change order form, and issue it to the contractor or supplier with a duplicate to the financial officer. Contractors and suppliers will have been warned in advance that no work should proceed nor should anything be purchased without a written authorization to do so. Although this all sounds a little cumbersome, it really is not. Without these safeguards, changes and additions could get out of hand and the company could be forced to spend sizable amounts of money without having had the opportunity to prejudge the effectiveness of the expenditures.

It is the construction manager or clerk of the works who will be doing the on-the-site supervision of construction and installation, making certain that the work is being accomplished in accordance with plans and specifications. Others should be participating in this effort, too. Periodic inspections should be made by each specialist whose specifications and recommendations are involved in the construction process. The inspection(s) should be scheduled, in each case, when construction or installation activity is at its peak in each specialist's field. Inspection should be made by the architect, the space planner, the interior designer, the audio-visual consultant, lighting consultant, and all others responsible for things built or installed. The construction manager should be present at all these inspections in order to activate any changes, corrections, mistakes, or additions that may require authorizations from the company.

The construction manager is the only one from whom the contractor may take orders and then only written, signed ones. It will, therefore, save time and energy and assure greater accuracy if the construction manager is part of each inspection. The project manager may do whatever inspecting he or she feels important to running the job, but must be available to help resolve unanticipated field conditions or any other problems as they arise, any time during the course of the building.

PUBLIC RELATIONS

It is during the period of construction that management can accomplish the major part of its in-house public relations, which was initially discussed in Chapter 4. By way of memos, newsletters, printed brochures, or company lectures, this is the time to begin or to step up the activity relative to the new company home and what it will mean to company personnel. In addition to discussing and describing the planned improvements in operations, organization, and staff amenities, the physical aspects of the new quarters (the building, the plan, design, colors, etc.) can be shared with the company people so that they can participate in the exciting adventure of relocation. Later, when the interior construction of the building has proceeded sufficiently, tours can be conducted and the space shown to those who will be living and working in it. Anything management can do to orient the employees to their new home will make the move that much more pleasant for everyone involved. The company can supply illustrated plans of the space, locating departments, services, and building facilities; maps of the area surrounding the site, showing where shopping, eating, and personal services are available; price ranges of neighborhood restaurants; and anything else that might be of interest to employees and help them find their way a little more comfortably.

If the move has been from one city to another, the same kind of information should be made available to the families that have relocated. They can be made to feel a little more at home with a guide to the new city, showing where they can shop, where the schools are located, where the houses of worship are, where the theatres and cultural centers are, what kind of social, cultural, educational, and recreational activities are available, where health and hospital facilities can be found, and everything anyone would want to know about the new locality that is to be called "home." An uprooted family goes through a major traumatic experience, and anything the company can do to make the transition easier will be of tremendous help to the employee and his or her family. It is worth spending time and money in that effort.

While on the subject of public relations, thought should be given to the things that should be done to announce the move to company friends and customers and certainly the government officials of the new locality. Public relations people will plan the eventual opening festivities, but it might be wise to lead up to the "office warming parties" with progress reports on construction and the move through personal and public news releases.

14 The Move

PREPARATIONS FOR THE MOVE

Personnel

The relocation of offices to a totally new geographic area means moving not only the company, but many of its people as well. The job of "people" relocation really begins very early in project development. It is, in fact, one of the cost items analyzed in the preliminary feasibility study. That analysis includes the dollars it will cost for severance pay for those employees who will not relocate, for the moving and related relocation expenses for those who will relocate, and for the fee to be paid to the real estate consultant who specializes in corporate personnel relocation.

The actual work involved in personnel relocation, although it starts early in the project, has not been described in detail up to now. But the end result, the move of people to their new homes, must coincide with the move of the company to its new home.

The work of the personnel relocation specialist begins in earnest right after the decision to relocate has been made. It starts with an analysis of company personnel policies and practices. If there are none relative to a move, the consultant will make recommendations concerning those that would apply to relocation and to the manner in which the company would underwrite such moves. The work requires a study of the projected housing markets in all areas close enough to the new offices to allow for commuting. It will include aid in the preparation of the relocation announcement to employees, the preparation and distribution of employee questionnaires, and the development of an employee advisory program. The consultant will analyze and tabulate questionnaire responses and prepare a report on the results of that analysis. From the indicated attrition, the expected relocation, and the required replacement of personnel at the new location, complete relocation cost estimates can be updated. After approval of this program, preparation can be made for relocation orientation and counseling meetings leading to the eventual acquisition of new homes and the disposition of existing ones.

Office

The company move, despite the hundreds of details that must be attended to, is purely and completely an exercise in logistics. In fact, the more military it is in its precision, the smoother the move will go. Preparation for the office move should also start early in the project but need not involve very many people at the beginning. It should start with a relatively small committee headed by the project manager or a top executive who will coordinate efforts with the project manager. It will be up to the project manager to make sure that any changes in schedule, anywhere along the line, will be made known to all project participants whose work will be affected by the changes. At the outset, the committee will consist of the chairman, the office manager (or someone who knows the total company operation), and an assistant who, hopefully, has had some experience working with moving companies.

The very first task of this committee will be the preparation of an overall moving plan. With the exception of the personnel relocation problems, this plan will detail the entire moving operation, listing everything that has to be done and setting up target dates for the accomplishment of each item. To prepare this detailed list, the committee should consult with each of the outside consultants that has been retained and with anyone inside the company who might conceivably add to the committee's knowledge of things to be done.

When everything has been duly listed, the committee can then begin to assign tasks to an expanded committee, delegating the duties and responsibilities necessary for accomplishing each and every listed item. How large the committee becomes depends entirely upon the size of the company—each department head can be a member (with or without assistants), or each floor can be represented on the committee. The size becomes a matter of judgment, based on the number of things to be done on the overall moving plan. Common sense dictates that the committee be kept as small as possible and that there be neither an overlap of duties nor any poorly defined areas of responsibilities. No matter what the size, on moving day someone (or two or three) must be at the space from which the company is moving and someone (or two or three) must be at the space to which the company is moving.

It will be extremely helpful if the company that will handle the move is chosen as
early as possible. This should not be done, however, until a determination has been made as to which presently owned furniture and equipment will be moved and reused in the new offices, what new furniture and equipment will be brought in by the suppliers, and what refurbished furniture will be carried to the new offices by the refinishers. Bids should then be solicited from movers and a company selected. Hired early, an experienced moving company can help organize the logistics of the move and advise the committee on its make-up and responsibilities.

Soliciting of "bids" from moving companies is not really an accurate description of the selection process. Moving fees (or tariffs) are set by regulatory bodies that determine and monitor rates for intra- and interstate moving, and there are no deviations permitted. So each company invited to "bid" will be judged by considerations other than just dollars. Each mover should be asked to tour the company space and study the total problem: What is to be moved, from where to where, what are the problems connected with getting things out of the building in which the company is presently located, what problems must be faced in getting things into the new building, and are there any odd and unusual problems connected with this particular move?

The creativity with which each mover plans to solve these problems, and what peripheral services each will perform to help the company make the move a smooth one, should be given more consideration in making a judgment about each moving company than the "guesstimates" on cost that each bidder will make. For example, when a company recently relocated from one state to another, one of the movers suggested that since all new files were being purchased for the new offices, the old files be emptied and left behind. The contents could be carted as paper instead of as furniture and that would mean using different equipment for which lower rates would prevail for that part of the move.

Each company making a bid should be asked to supply the following information with their written, submitted proposal: the location of their major and satellite garages, the number and type of trucks owned, the availability to the company of other equipment that might be needed, the number of full-time employees and their lengths of service, the experience of their supervisory personnel, the applicable tariffs, number of people to be used on the job, insurance coverage, union affiliations, moves handled similar to this one, performance and credit references, and additional services that will be performed as part of this job. The additional services could include giving instructions to relocating company personnel with packing hints and hints about the disposal of "squirreled" material that should be thrown out rather than moved, supplying disposal containers, tagging all items to be moved, and marking them for locations in the new quarters.

After a moving company has been chosen, there should be no hesitancy about calling upon their people for help and advice. An experienced representative of a moving company should be able to approve and improve the overall plan, help to coordinate and schedule the company effort, and suggest the number of company people who might be required to implement the moving plan. Since staff and moving company people will have to work together, it is wise to ask the moving company representative to sit in on all moving committee meetings. Also, because the space planner and designer know a good deal about what has been arranged and about what will be moved, it is wise to take advantage of their familiarity with the project and with the new quarters and ask them to be available to the committee for consultation.

The overall plan, or checklist of things to be done, should have three separate and distinct parts to it: Things to be done (1) before the move, (2) as part of the move, and (3) after the move. Each list should describe the things to be accomplished, the person or persons assigned to the task, the date assigned, the target date for completion, and the actual completion date. Each task will be assigned to the individual or group most capable of handling it, i.e., a member of the committee, the moving company, the space planner, the interior designer, or anyone else who should logically be assigned that particular job.

Those things to be accomplished *before the move* include the following:

- Select a moving committee. There can be two target dates for this: one at the outset, when a basic committee can be selected, and the other right after the operation plan has been approved, when a full committee can be organized. By knowing the extent of the operational plan it will be easier to determine the size of the full committee.

- Select a mover.

- Obtain furniture and equipment plans of the new space and give copies to the mover. The plans should show both new furniture that will be brought in by suppliers and existing furniture and equipment to be carried by the movers.

- Schedule moving date(s).

- Send moving notices with new address, telephone number, and other pertinent information to:

  Clients
  Suppliers
  Post office
  Magazines
  Newspapers
  Banks
  Insurance companies
  Government regulatory agencies

- Arrange for a change of listing in the telephone directory.

- Arrange for listings in the directory of the new building.

- Order new stationery—letterheads, cards, checks, invoices, forms, and anything else that carries the company address and telephone number.

- Conduct a throwaway campaign. All personnel should be asked, kidded, and cajoled to throw out items they will not be needing. Disposal bins should be strategically placed so that tossing things away is made as easy as possible. Graphics should be placed around the premises urging people to join this "throwaway campaign."

- Check insurance coverage. The company might want additional insurance to augment that carried by the moving company.
- Check the necessity for security guards. Stored furniture may have to be guarded or a security identification system set up during the normally confusing time of the move. The presence of guards could lessen the need for more insurance or, at least, reduce the insurance cost.

The things to be done *for the move* include the following:

- Schedule removal of furniture and equipment for refurbishing and schedule its delivery to the new offices.
- Select personnel to oversee removal from existing offices.
- Select personnel to oversee receipt of all moved items at the new quarters and set up a "headquarters station."
- Check on the delivery of new furniture to the new quarters.
- Schedule a delivery to the old office of cartons, boxes, wardrobes, and other containers provided by the moving company.
- Tag all furniture and equipment and use the furniture plan code for location delivery to new offices.
- Assign packing tasks.
- Schedule packing and distribute instructions to those responsible for it. The moving company should provide complete packing instructions, including how to disconnect machines and typewriters that may be fastened to work surfaces, how to empty shelves of books and papers, what to pack in desk drawers and what not to pack in them, what to do with clocks, small pictures, liquids, perfumes, glue and ink, what to leave on the walls and what to remove, and what to do with pens, pencils, and paper clips.
- Install directional and area identification signs in the new offices.
- Arrange for telephone hook-up between the old and the new premises.
- Arrange for elevator service in both buildings on moving day.
- Protect elevator cabs, lobbies, walls, and floors from damage during the move-in.
- Schedule telephone installers to stand by during the move. Last-minute changes and additions and corrections should be attended to before the start of business after the move-in.
- Install a lost-and-found department on the new premises. All company personnel and movers should know exactly where it is located.
- Instruct each person in the company concerning his or her individual responsibility for housekeeping his or her area.

The things to be done *after the move* include the following:

- Schedule staff work for getting files, shelves, and supplies set up as rapidly as possible. Tags should be removed from all furniture and equipment.

- Thoroughly clean the premises. This should be done before the start of business in the new offices, hopefully with everything shelved, filed, and in drawers, with boxes, cartons, and bins removed.

- Test all systems and procedures. Word processing, records management systems, telephones, and all other systems and procedures changes must now go through their "shakedown" testing period. Further training of personnel and/or systems managers may be indicated before testing is complete and the systems considered satisfactory. Operations' manuals should be prepared to guide staff and managers and to provide a ready reference, should problems arise.

- Building maintenance and cleaning services procedures should be tested. Operations' manuals should be prepared, outlining all normal procedures as well as all foreseeable emergencies. Details of maintenance and cleaning are described at the end of this chapter.

- Prepare a list of items to be completed. These "punch lists" will include items still remaining to be done or to be furnished by the general contractor or the subcontractors. A second list will itemize the furniture, furnishings, or equipment not yet delivered or installed or damaged in delivery. The lists should show what has to be done, who is responsible for doing it, and who is responsible for seeing that it gets done.

- Prepare a list of additional furniture, furnishings, and equipment items requested by company personnel. After every move, requests are made for things needed or believed to be needed. These things include bookcases, chairs, shelving, calculators, and even typewriters. In many cases, the requests are valid but, valid or not, an orderly procedure should be set up to determine what should not be purchased. Except in an emergency, nothing in the way of additional equipment should be purchased until all requests have been received and the total costs examined and approved by management. Without such a procedure, extra costs could get completely out of hand. One way of gathering the requests would be by sending out a questionnaire, asking each employee to list any furniture, furnishings, or equipment that each believes would help in the performance of his or her job. Visits could then be made by the project manager or the interior designer to each person making a request and the need for the item checked. Cost sheets would then be prepared for the purchase or design and fabrication of the needed items, with the costs submitted to management for approval.

  A more satisfactory method, however, would be to conduct a space audit to find out not only what items are needed but how effective the entire relocation has been for each person and each department. An audit of this kind should not be conducted until some time has elapsed after occupancy. It certainly should not be done until the company has lived in its new quarters for at least 3 to 6 months. The audit would be conducted by the project manager or someone from his or her staff and the space planner with the interior designer. They would visit all company personnel. Department heads would be questioned about the operation of their departments in the new quarters and about any unexpected problems that may have arisen. At the same time, each person would be questioned about his or her equipment needs. The list of items requested should be about the same no matter which method is used for gathering the information. The space audit, however, could pick up problems that might otherwise take time to find and solve. A recent audit showed that the medical department of a relocated company was getting far more legitimate use than had been anticipated. They really needed more space but did not know what they could do about it. At the same time, a sales department which had planned for growth was going to get smaller because of an unexpected product-line curtailment. This fortuitous set of circumstances allowed for a swap of space, although a costly one because of the electrical and plumbing changes that had to be made to accommodate the medical department. If the sales department had not provided the needed space, the audit, having revealed the need, would have indicated how imperative it was that space be found for the medical department somewhere, somehow. In any event, nothing was ordered from the list of requested furniture and equipment, nor was construction begun for the medical and sales departments, until all costs had been gathered and management had approved the total expenditure.

One last word about the move itself: Because the efficiency of the move depends so much on timetable accuracy, bottlenecks anywhere along the way can cause serious and unnecessary delays. The order in which departments or sections of departments move must be plotted to avoid traffic jams at doorways, corridors, elevators, stairwells, and loading docks in both the old and the new premises. These jam-ups can waste time, damage equipment, and frazzle nerves. After all the weeks and months and sometimes years of planning, it is a shame to allow avoidable mishaps to mar what should be an exciting and productive experience.

AFTER THE MOVE—PROTECTING THE INVESTMENT

It would be an even greater shame if the major investment made to bring this project to fruition went unprotected because of poor or insufficient maintenance. If the space is rented and the landlord is responsible for building maintenance and cleaning services, there is always something special that requires attention and that will have to be done at the tenant's expense. If it is a building constructed for single occupancy, to be owned and operated by the occupying company (or leased and operated by the occupying company), then all building maintenance and cleaning services become company responsibility.

In the case of rented space, it is not unusual for the company to have to contract separately for bulb-replacements, fixture washing, and the washing of all interior glass partitions. In order to find out exactly what the company has to do, a list of cleaning and maintenance needs should be prepared (a fairly comprehensive list is given below) and then compared to the items the landlord has agreed to take care of under the terms of the lease. In most cases whatever additional services are needed can be obtained through the landlord. In a multiple-occupancy building those same services would probably be required by other tenants and could certainly be supplied by the company already retained to give basic services. It should be possible to save some money in equipment carting and supply procurement if the tenants use the same service companies already working in the building.

In a company-owned building, building maintenance and office cleaning are both the owner's responsibility. Included in this would be the security systems and the security guards, the elevator starters, and the information clerks.

Building maintenance includes the care of:

- Electricity, water, and gas systems
- Elevators and escalators
- Heating, ventilating, and air conditioning systems
- Material-handling systems
- Security systems including sprinklers, fire extinguishers, hoses, fire and theft detection devices, emergency lighting, and locks and keys

Building repair includes:

- Patching walls and ceilings
- Repairing building carpeting, doors, locks, windows, and blinds
- Replacing floor tiles and window panes

Building cleaning includes:

- Care of plantings, both inside and out
- Lavatories and janitors' closets
- Maintaining lobby, elevators, and the building directory
- Stairwells and corridors
- Ventilating filters
- Walkways, driveways, and parking areas (including snow removal)
- Washing windows

Office cleaning includes:

- Cleaning drinking fountains

- Dusting furniture and equipment

- Emptying ash trays, sand urns, and waste baskets

- Sweeping and mopping resilient flooring

- Vacuuming carpets, draperies, and upholstered furniture

- Washing glass partitions

In addition to all these things a timetable should be prepared for the regular care of everything requiring scheduled maintenance. These would be things done once a week, once a month, twice a year, or annually. The frequency would be a matter dictated mainly by experience and would vary considerably with climate, environmental problems or pollution, and traffic by and through the building. Not all these things would be done by the staff. For example, drapery cleaning would be done off the premises by a dry cleaning or laundry process. In all probability it would be handled by the company that made the drapes and that would rehang them after the cleaning. The scheduled items should include:

- Buffing and waxing resilient flooring

- Cleaning and conservation of art

- Cleaning draperies and carpets

- Cleaning lighting fixtures

- Cleaning venetian blinds

- Dusting books

- Painting touch-up and repainting

- Polishing metal

- Polishing wood furniture

- Servicing potted plants

- Washing tile and marble walls

Office repairing would include furniture, furnishings and equipment broken or damaged in use, such as:

- Desks or file drawers

- Cabinet doors

- Furniture legs, seats, or backs

- Shelving

- Swivel chairs and casters

If maintenance and cleaning is to be a staff effort, a list must be prepared and an inventory kept of all required supplies. This should start with basic equipment such as vacuum cleaners (or hose fittings if there is a building vacuum system), floor cleaning, sanding and waxing machines, buckets, mop wringers, brooms, mops and ladders, plus the disposable items such as dust cloths, detergents, soaps, waxes, toilet tissues, paper towels, and all the other things needed to "run a home."

The *public relations* input, which started when the staff was first told about the move and continued with all the "bulletins" that kept the staff informed of progress, will continue past the move-in through the day when the space is opened to the public. The public relations people initially prepared and presented neighborhood and community information to aid employees and their families get to know their locality. They should also prepare, in whatever form would be best, a bill of particulars concerning the "care and feeding" of the new quarters. Such instructions should be a continuation of the description of the comforts being provided, the art program being inaugurated, and the things that are expected of the staff to help keep up the quality of the new space. It should list the things that may and may not be done by way of personal decorating, the ways by which individual areas should be kept neat and orderly, and the desirability for the staff to have its own early warning system of furniture or equipment breakdowns or maintenance deficiencies. In the same bill of particulars, the staff should be told what each is expected to do in community activities such as fire drills and given dining and recreation schedules.

Some part of the public relations effort will be aimed at people outside of the company itself. How much or how little will depend upon the target(s) of that effort. In all probability it would have started at the time the decision to move was made with preliminary announcements to the media, both public and trade, followed by progress reports up to and including the move.

What happens from then on will depend upon company policy and the creativity of the public relations people. Any one of several of the following things can be included in the effort, and each can be as simple or extravagant as the company desires: mailed announcements of the change of address and telephone number; stories and photographs in newspapers, trade media, business magazines, design magazines, and office procedure magazines; a press party; an employee party; a friends and customers party (these parties can be combined and they can be with or without community and local government participation); conducted tours; an introduction to and a tour of the facilities open to the community such as auditorium and exhibition space.

Now that the company fully occupies its space, there is no reason at all why it should not show off the result of the time, energy, and creativity that went into the planning and building of this home of the future.

Section V: Project Staffing

ACCOUNTING

The accounting department of the relocating company should be part of the project from the beginning. Its real work will begin when purchasing and construction actually get underway. Because of details involved in auditing a complex project, it would be best to have one member of the department made responsible for handling the details and the procedures to be followed. That person should have copies of the first analysis of costs that were prepared with the feasibility studies, a complete history of the budget, and the changes that have occurred from the beginning, and should prepare a schedule of all contractual commitments and all purchase orders in order to anticipate and prepare to meet all obligations. He or she will pay all requisitions and invoices that have been properly approved, question all discrepancies from anticipated costs, and withhold percentages agreed upon until the completion and final billing on each phase of the work; will audit all time sheets of those consultants whose effort is being measured on a time basis and all requisitions for reimbursement of out-of-pocket and travel expense; and should also keep an accurate and timely record of dollar commitments, accounts payable, and the disbursements made to date. These figures should be reconciled with the latest approved budget and with the approvals given for all changes and additions made as the job progresses.

INSURANCE ADVISOR

Additional insurance may be required because of the relocation. Most companies have their own insurance broker or advisor, who is the one to provide help. Although the general contractor, suppliers, and moving companies will have their own insurance coverage, all facets of the problem must be examined and the adequacy of their coverage accepted or augmented. Some of the special areas of coverage are:

- Damage to surrounding buildings and property within them because of blasting or foundation installation
- Bodily injury to workers, supervisory personnel, and consultants' supervisors
- Construction errors
- Damage by fire to construction and material
- Theft of construction material and supplies
- Fire and theft of stored furniture, furnishings, and equipment both on and off the premises, prior to installation
- Loss or damage to furniture, furnishings, and equipment en route to new premises

SECURITY GUARDS

Security guards may be needed to prevent pilferage during the confusion of moving. They can also be hired on a 24-hour-a-day basis if much furniture and equipment is installed or stored in the new premises before the company actually occupies the space. Guards may conceivably be needed to patrol all building entrances and exits and act as visitor controls, issuing passes and conducting visitors to their destinations. They can be salaried employees or the employees of an outside service company retained to supply security help.

In addition to determining security guard needs, it would be wise to have the insurance advisor analyze their impact on insurance rates.

Possible sources for security guards include:

- *Security Management*
  200 K Street N.W.
  Washington, D.C. 20006
- Recommendations
- Yellow Pages

MOVERS

The movers' work is tied directly to the company moving committee. Because of this, what they must do, how the job is to be awarded, and how the fees are determined have all been described in Chapter 14. No further clarification is needed here.

Possible sources for movers include:

- Recommendations
- Yellow Pages

BUILDING MAINTENANCE

Building maintenance takes on more than casual importance only if the building is company-owned or company-managed. The work itself can be done by a company retained for that purpose, by an in-house staff, or by a house staff aided by outside specialists in various fields. In any case, there should be one company employee in charge of the building and its maintenance. By whatever title, superintendent, manager of building operations, or vice president of building operations, this employee would be responsible for overseeing the retained service company or the in-house crew to make sure that all building systems are operating at peak efficiency. Hopefully, the manager will have wide experience in engineering, construction, and building maintenance.

If a service company is to handle all maintenance work, their credentials (experience, staff size, supervisors' knowledge and length of service with the company, performance on similar projects as measured by users' references, insurance coverage, and financial stability) should be very carefully checked. The same kind of checking should be done for any companies retained, even if only for very special tasks such as air conditioning and elevator repairs and maintenance.

An in-house crew can include a chief engineer, electrician(s), mechanics capable of tending to all but major repairs of building equipment, plumbing and electrical work, and porters. Elevator starters, information clerks, and security guards can also be under the supervision of the operations manager.

The in-house crew should be salaried personnel. Prevailing wages for each work category are available from the local Building Owners and Managers Association, from the local Real Estate Board, or from the locals of the various unions involved. Any outside services should be retained on a cost-plus or flat-fee-per-job basis.

Sources are listed under "Cleaning Services."

CLEANING SERVICES

These services, like building maintenance, can be handled by an in-house staff, a service company, or a combination of the two. The responsibility for overseeing the work can be assigned to the operations manager, and the staff can, in fact, be part of the operations department.

A retained service company can handle the total job, supplying all the necessary skills including housekeeper supervision, window washing, fixture cleaning, bulb replacement, etc. An in-house staff should consist of a housekeeper, cleaning staff, floor buffer, and waxers, etc. Most in-house staffs do not do the window washing, fixture cleaning, or bulb replacement. These and similar jobs should be contracted for through an outside service.

An in-house staff is salaried while outside services are paid a cost plus or a fixed fee. Possible sources for building maintenance and cleaning services include:

- *Buildings*
  427 Sixth Avenue S.E.
  Cedar Rapids, Iowa 52406

- *Building Operating Management*
  Box 694
  407 E. Michigan Street
  Milwaukee, Wisconsin 53201

- *Building Owner and Manager*
  1221 Massachusettss Avenue N.W.
  Washington, D.C. 20005

PUBLIC RELATIONS

Public relations is another service sometimes handled in-house, sometimes by an outside firm, and sometimes by a combination of the two. As a rule, a large company will have an in-house staff to handle the public relations work that comes up day-to-day for stockholders, the investment community, internal communication, or product news. But, inside or out, public relations work, described at length throughout the book, will play a vital part throughout the project.

Public relations firms' charges are either on a yearly retainer or on a fee for a particular job. Travel and out-of-pocket expenses as well as any printing costs are billed separately.

Possible sources for public relations talent include:

- Recommendations
- Public Relations Society of America
  845 Third Avenue
  New York, New York 10022

Appendix 1: Relocation Action List

The list which follows is a summary of the things that have been discussed in this book. The compilation has been made in order to provide the user with a comprehensive checklist of the areas to be covered in a relocation project. Not all listed items will be relevant to each project, in not all projects will it be possible to maintain the chronological sequence suggested by the list, nor will all projects allow the luxury of time that should be available under ideal circumstances. Each user will, therefore, have to edit the list to fit the problem—just as each user will have to assign the responsibility for each item on the list according to the talents available.

It is important to remember that before beginning work on each phase, the steps to be taken in that phase should be studied to: (1) clearly determine the work to be done, (2) identify the staff members and outside consultants that will be used, (3) allot the tasks to be performed, (4) prepare the required forms and questionnaires for work evaluation and financial analysis, and (5) prepare the controls to be used on time and dollar expenditures.

Remember, too, that the first section of this checklist deals with those things to be done for the feasibility study. This effort will determine whether or not the project will actually proceed. If it will, all the work done in this study will be done again—in much greater depth and detail.

PHASE I—FEASIBILITY STUDY

A. Survey existing organization.

   1. Inventory existing space.

   2. Prepare growth projection chart.

   3. Assess existing real estate ownerships and/or leases.

   4. Analyze the present building.

   a. Quality.

   b. Neighborhood.

   c. Availability to staff and clients.

   d. Geographical location (i.e., city, state, region).

   5. Analyze the efficiency of existing space.

   a. Layout.

   b. Ability to accommodate growth.

   c. Space standards.

   6. Evaluate the impact of space appearance on staff and public.

B. Survey possible changes. (This should start with executive orientation meeting to discuss goals for all the changes that might be made.)

   1. Study organization changes.

   a. Departments.

   b. Service areas.

   2. Study operation changes.

   a. Systems and procedures.

   b. Equipment improvement.

   3. Study possible new facilities and amenities.

   4. Study changes in space use.

   a. Space concepts.

   b. Space standards.

   c. New work stations and/or furniture.

C. Survey choices for physical change.

   1. Location.

   2. Evaluate methods to accomplish housing.

   a. Rent.

   b. Build.

    c. Renovate.

    d. Redecorate.

D. Determine feasibility of project.

  1. Tabulate number of square feet required.

  2. Prepare complete financial analysis.

  3. Evaluate advantages and disadvantages of relocation or renovation.

PHASE II—PLANNING

A. Departments and service areas.

  1. Tour space with staff and consultants.

  2. Inform company personnel of plans.

  3. Inventory all furniture and equipment.

  4. Analyze all leases, real estate ownerships, options, etc.

  5. Interview all department and service area heads.

  6. Conduct traffic studies.

  7. List all possible new facilities.

B. Operations.

  1. Study paper management.

    a. Word processing.

    b. Records management.

    c. Prepare operations manual.

  2. Analyze supply problems.

    a. Purchasing.

    b. Storage.

    c. Distribution.

  3. Review data processing.

    a. Equipment.

    b. Physical requirements.

- Space.
- Flooring.
- Air conditioning.
- Fire controls.
- Security.

4. Study communications problems.

   a. Telephone.

   b. Intercom.

   c. Audio-visual.

5. Evaluate company services.

   a. Conference/meeting rooms.

   b. Library.

   c. Special-use rooms.

6. Determine security policies.

   a. Personnel.

   b. Corporate.

   c. Building.

C. Personnel.

  1. Determine company policy on:

    a. Operational considerations.

- Interview rooms.
- Medical department.
- Dining facilities.
- Recreation.
- Travel aid.
- Security.
- Others.

    b. Environmental considerations.

- Lighting.
- Acoustics.
- Work stations.
- Furniture and furnishings.
- Others.

    c. Sociological considerations.

D. Space.

  1. Survey space concepts.

    a. Conventional plan.

      b. Modified conventional plan.

      c. Open plan.

   2. Analyze impact of new space standards.

   3. Analyze special requirements for space-taking equipment.

   4. Analyze anticipated growth.

   5. Tabulate space needs for a given time in periodic increments

   6. Prepare profile of hypothetical building to indicate department.

   7. Prepare departmental space studies on floor plan of hypothetical building.

E. Finances and reports.

   1. Update all budget estimates.

   2. Analyze changes in costs.

   3. Report recommendations to management on:

      a. New procedures.

      b. Standards.

      c. Facilities.

      d. Equipment.

      e. Plan concepts.

      f. Others.

PHASE III—APPLYING THE PLAN

A. Explore real estate alternatives.

   1. Recommend use and/or disposal of owned and leased space.

      a. Estimate possible profit or loss from these recommendations.

   2. Determine location for the company offices through study of:

      a. Corporate needs.

      b. Work force availability.

      c. Transportation.

      d. Zoning.

      e. Taxes.

      f. Housing for personnel.

      g. Others.

   3. Analyze possibility of renting.

  a. Compare available buildings.

  - Location.

  - Floor size.

  - HVAC.

  - Electricity.

  - Elevators.

  - Toilets.

  - Ceiling heights.

  - Floor loads.

  - Others.

  b. Prepare leases.

  c. Prepare work letter.

  d. Negotiate rents and work.

4. Analyze possibility of building.

  a. Single or multiple occupancy?

  b. One building or campus configuration of several buildings?

  c. Prepare list of desirable features for inclusion in new building(s).

  d. Determine all interior and exterior design aims and requirements.

5. Analyze renovation or redecoration.

  a. List all building elements that should be renovated.

  b. List all interior office areas that should be renovated.

  c. List all interior office areas that should be redecorated.

PHASE IV—DEVELOPING THE PLAN

A. Program space needs.

B. Plan the building.

  1. Test the interaction of space and building plans.

C. Conduct design meeting.

D. Update the budget estimates.

E. Prepare design presentation.

  1. Consult with specialists on lighting, accoustics, flooring, etc.

F. Determine methods for bidding:

  1. Competitive.

2. Negotiated.

G. Prepare construction documents:

    1. Working drawings.

    2. Specifications.

    3. Documents for bidders.

PHASE V—IMPLEMENTING THE PLAN

A. Construction.

    1. Coordinate delivery of material, furniture, furnishings, etc.

    2. Coordinate progress of building.

    3. Audit all requisitions and final bills.

B. Move-in.

    1. Arrange for public relations indoctrination for:

        a. Company personnel and their families.

        b. Clients.

        c. General public.

        d. Local governing bodies.

    2. Set up moving committee to handle details before, during, and after the move.

    3. Select mover to handle company and employee's moves.

    4. Coordinate installation of furniture and equipment.

    5. Coordinate installation of systems and procedures and training of management personnel and staff in systems operation.

    6. Hire crews for and schedule:

        a. Building maintenance.

            • Utility systems.

            • Elevators and escalators.

            • HVAC.

            • Material-handling systems.

            • Security systems.

        b. Building repair.

        c. Cleaning.

            • Building.

            • Offices.

Appendix 2: For Your Information

The list of associations, books, and magazines which follows is a guide to some (but certainly not all) of the sources of information available to those readers anxious to know more about the many aspects of relocation. Where the specific field of knowledge is not obviously indicated by the name of the source, a parenthetical explanation is added.

ASSOCIATIONS

Acoustical Society of America
335 East 45th Street
New York, New York 10017

Administrative Management Society
Maryland Road
Willow Grove, Pennsylvania 19090
(Will supply information on any aspects of office management, systems and procedures)

American Institute of Architects
1735 New York Avenue N.W.
Washington, D.C. 20006

American Institute of Management
125 East 38th Street
New York, New York 10016

American Management Association
135 West 50th Street
New York, New York 10020
(In addition to conducting seminars on all subjects related to office planning, the association publishes books and other literature)

Association of Records Managers and Administration
P.O. Box 281
Bradford, Rhode Island 02808

American Society for Industrial Security
2000 K Street N.W.
Washington, D.C. 20006

American Society of Civil Engineers
345 East 47th Street
New York, New York 10017
(Electrical, electronic, air conditioning, and illuminating engineering, among others)

American Society of Interior Designers
730 Fifth Avenue
New York, New York 10019

Art Dealers Association of America
575 Madison Avenue
New York, New York 10022

Audio Engineering Society
60 East 42d Street
New York, New York 10017

Building Owners and Managers Association
1221 Massachusetts Avenue N.W.
Washington, D.C. 20005

Carpet and Rug Institute
P.O. Box 2048
Dalton, Georgia 30720

Illuminating Engineering Society
345 East 47th Street
New York, New York 10017

Industrial Designers Society of America
1750 Old Meadow Road
McLean, Virginia 22101
(Information on design for the handicapped)

Institute for Professional Education
1901 North Ft. Myer Drive
Arlington, Virginia 22209
(Information on word processing, microfilming and data processing)

Institute of Business Designers
1350 Avenue of the Americas
New York, New York 10019

Institute of Electrical and Electronics Engineers
345 East 47th Street
New York, New York 10017

Institute of Management Consultants
347 Madison Avenue
New York, New York 10017

International Audiovisual Society
P.O. Box 54; Cullowhee
North Carolina 28723

National Council of Acoustical Consultants
8811 Colesville Road
Silver Spring, Maryland 20910

National Fire Protection Association
470 Atlantic Avenue
Boston, Massachusetts 02110

National Records Management Council
60 East 42d Street
New York, New York 10017

Public Relations Society of America
845 Third Avenue
New York, New York 10022

Society of Professional Management Consultants
205 West 89th Street
New York, New York 10024

BOOKS

A Complete Guide to Building & Plant Maintenance
Sack, Thomas F.: Prentice-Hall, 1971

Communications System Design
Panter, Philip F.: McGraw-Hill, 1972

Cost Effective Telecommunications
Kuehn, Richard A.: Amacom, 1975

Handbook of Modern Office Management & Administrative Services
Heyel, Carl (ed.): McGraw-Hill, 1972

Office Administration Handbook
Edited by Dartnell Corporation

Office Planning and Design
Saphier, Michael: McGraw-Hill, 1969

Planning the Office Landscape
Palmer, Alvin E., and M. Susan Lewis: McGraw-Hill, 1977

Profit Through Design
Mogulescu, Maurice: Amacom, 1970

Records Management
Benedon, William: Prentice-Hall, 1969

Records Management Step by Step
Blegen, August H.: Office Publications, 1965

Selecting, Planning, and Managing Office Space
Robichaud, Beryl: McGraw-Hill, 1958

Word Processing
Anderson, Thomas J., and William R. Trotter: Amacom, 1974

SECURITY

Books, magazines, and pamphlets on the subject published by Security World Publishing Company (see address below)

Other publishing sources:

Amacom (Division of American Management Association)
135 West 50th Street
New York, New York 10020

Dartnell Corporation
4660 Ravenswood Avenue
Chicago, Illinois 60640

McGraw-Hill Book Company
1221 Avenue of the Americas
New York, New York 10020

Office Publications, Inc.
1200 Summer Street
Stamford, Connecticut 06904

Prentice-Hall, Inc.
Route 9W, Englewood Cliffs
New Jersey 07632

Security World Publishing Co., Inc.
2639 South La Cienega Boulevard
Los Angeles, California 90034

Administrative Management
51 Madison Avenue
New York, New York 10010
*(Articles on planning, design, systems and procedures, comparative analysis of office
equipment, etc.)*

Architectural Record
1221 Avenue of the Americas
New York, New York 10020

Audio Video
380 Madison Avenue
New York, New York 10017

Building Operating Management
Box 694, 407 East Michigan Street
Milwaukee, Wisconsin 53201

Building Owner and Manager
1221 Massachusetts Avenue N.W.
Washington, D.C. 20005

Buildings
427 Sixth Avenue S.E.
Cedar Rapids, Iowa 52406

Communications
1900 West Yale
Englewood, Colorado 80110

Contract
1515 Broadway
New York, New York 10036
*(Articles on office planning, furniture, furnishings, space concepts, etc.; also publishes
an annual directory of sources of furniture and furnishings)*

The Designer Magazine
1010 Third Avenue
New York, New York 10021

Engineering News Record
1221 Avenue of the Americas
New York, New York 10020

Food & Equipment Product News
347 Madison Avenue
New York, New York 10017

Information & Records Management
250 Fulton Avenue
Hempstead, New York 11550

Industrial Design
1 Astor Plaza
New York, New York 10036
(Information on design for the handicapped)

Interior Design
150 East 58th Street
New York, New York 10022
(Also publishes an annual directory of sources of furniture and furnishings)

Interiors
1 Astor Plaza
New York, New York 10036

Journal of Systems Management
24587 Bagley Road
Cleveland, Ohio 44138

Management World
Maryland Road
Willow Grove, Pennsylvania 19090

Modern Office Procedures
614 Superior Avenue West
Cleveland, Ohio 44113

The Office
1200 Summer Street
Stamford, Connecticut 06904

Office Product News
645 Stewart Avenue
Garden City, New York 11530

Progressive Architecture
600 Summer Street
Stamford, Connecticut 06904

Reproductions Review & Methods
401 North Broad Street
Philadelphia, Pennsylvania 19108

Security Management
2000 K Street N.W.
Washington, D.C. 20006

Telecommunications
610 Washington Street
Dedham, Massachusetts 02026

Word Processing World
51 Madison Avenue
New York, New York 10010

Index

Index